THE
JAPANDI
HOME

Nordic Minimalism Meets
Japanese Zen

CATE ST HILL

THE
JAPANDI
HOME

Nordic Minimalism Meets
Japanese Zen

U

**UNION
SQUARE
& CO.**

NEW YORK

U

**UNION
SQUARE
& CO.**

NEW YORK

UNION SQUARE & CO. and the distinctive
Union Square & Co. logo are trademarks of
Sterling Publishing Co., Inc.

Union Square & Co., LLC, is a subsidiary of
Sterling Publishing Co., Inc.

Text © 2025 Cate St Hill

ISBN 978-1-4549-5819-2

For information about custom editions, special sales, and premium
purchases, please contact specialsales@unionsquareandco.com.

Printed in China.

10 9 8 7 6 5 4 3 2 1

unionsquareandco.com

Designer: Sarah Pyke
Senior Designer: Rachel Cross
Art Director: Gemma Wilson
Picture Research: Claire Holland
Project Editor: Blanche Craig
Copy Editor: Ruth Patrick
Production Manager: David Hearn
Commissioning Editor: Lily de Gatacre
Managing Editor: Emma Harverson
Associate Publisher: Eszter Karpati
Publisher: Lorraine Dickey

CONTENTS

Introduction

The styles of Japanese and Scandinavian design have become so intertwined that it is often hard to know where one ends and the other begins. A match made in an aesthete's heaven, together they stand for the same mindful, considered values and share the same calm, minimalist aesthetic. But these two worlds have been united in mutual collaboration and respect for centuries, far preceding the concept of Japandi as "a popular design style."

The story begins long before there was even the notion of design as we know it now. Here we have two regions on opposite sides of the world: one a rugged peninsula made up of dramatic fjords, alpine mountains, lakes, and thousands of small islands; the other a vast archipelago that stretches from the subarctic in the north to the subtropical in the south. Both are covered in a heavily forested landscape, and subject to an unpredictable climate and long, cold winters that dictate a more insular way of life. In many ways, both came to be the introverts of the world—the Nordic countries learning to be self-sufficient and thrive in a harsh setting, and Japan for a long time shielding itself from the world to protect its identity and survival. This created fertile grounds for the development of two distinct, yet not completely dissimilar, cultural identities, with the space and freedom to work with nature and refine crafts, techniques, and traditions.

The first wave of collective intrigue arrived when Japan came out of a long period of national isolation, transitioning from a secluded, secretive country that banned foreign travel to a modern destination, trading goods, products, and ideas with the world. For more than two hundred years, up until the mid-1850s, Japan was closed off to the world through the policy of *sakoku* ("closed country"), fearing the influence of European beliefs and possible social unrest. Christianity was outlawed, foreign books were forbidden, and entry was limited to only the Dutch and Chinese. It was the Americans who finally forced Japan reluctantly back into trade in 1853. Once travel restrictions were lifted, European voyagers, including those from Denmark and Sweden, couldn't contain their curiosity for a faraway country that appeared so mysteriously unlike them. Just like the Grand Tours of Italy in the 18th century, writers, artists, and collectors would travel to Japan in search of antiquities, objects, and artifacts to bring back home. Japanese woodcuts, screens, paintings, and ceramics all became collectible items.

Interest piqued with the Paris Exposition of 1867—a world fair used to showcase technological innovations and industrial prowess as well as the fine arts—when Japan exhibited for the very first time with a replica of a Japanese house. The word "Japonisme" was coined by French art critic Philippe Burty to

describe the complete infatuation the West had with Japanese art and design. As American art historian Gabriel P. Weisberg writes in the book *Japanomania in the Nordic Countries, 1875–1918*, "Japonisme was everywhere; it was appreciated as a fad, a cult and a basic quality of modernism." Nordic artists based in Paris picked up on this trend and Japanese aesthetics soon infiltrated everything from modern painting—inspiring asymmetrical compositions, unusual perspectives, flat surfaces, and muted colors—to ceramics, furniture designs, and interior decoration. The humble simplicity of Japanese design had a refreshing appeal, contrasting with the stuffy fashions of the time that relied on dark, heavy furniture and excessive ornamentation. In 1903, the German–Japanese critic Sadakichi Hartmann wrote, "The Japanese ... have also taught us simplicity in domestic surroundings. They have shown us that a room needs not to be a museum in order to make an artistic impression; that true elegance lies in simplicity."

Architecturally, the Japanese influence can be seen in low-rise Scandi homes designed in the mid-20th century with open floor plans and a dominant use of wood. Yoshida Tetsurō's seminal book *The Japanese House* from 1935, acted as a guide to traditional Japanese architecture for Nordic architects, inspiring the likes of Finnish architect Alvar Aalto to integrate features such as room dividers and uninterrupted views of nature into their designs. Meanwhile, the Danish masters of modernism were adopting the Japanese material palette—Kaare Klint making pleated paper lampshades, Arne Jacobsen using bamboo as cladding and to make easy chairs, and Poul Kjærholm creating undulating Japanese-style wooden screens. Before long, Scandinavian and Japanese design became so blended, it was hard to tell them apart.

But Japonisme wasn't just a one-way street—Nordic ideals of simplicity and functionality were also brought to Japan. Western-style interiors intrigued a nation that was used to a floor-level lifestyle. Seeking to respond to the appetite for modern Western trends and boost international trading, influential European designers—including Kaj Franck, one of the leading figures of Finnish design—were invited over by the Japanese government as special advisors to help improve Japan's design industry. Their role was to share their skills and expertise so that Japan could ultimately make products for the West. German designer Bruno Taut and French designer Charlotte Perriand, were also brought on board in the 1930s and '40s, the inspiration from Japan clear to see in their later work. Franck himself was one of several designers who won the Lunning Prize, a travel scholarship awarded to eminent Nordic designers from 1951 to 1970 with the aim of promoting Scandinavian design abroad.

Having never really had the need to make tables and chairs on a mass scale before, the Japanese had a lot to learn from the Scandinavians—the world experts in furniture design—if they were to catch up with the rest of the globe and compete for goods. It was a mutually beneficial relationship—the Scandinavians would typically present their designs and give lectures, while at the same time gaining an insight into Japanese craft. In return, the Japanese government would also send apprentices and students over to the Nordic countries to learn about Scandinavian design. Japan and Scandinavia's reputation for world-class craftsmanship was sealed. Today, contemporary Japanese manufacturers, such as Koyori and Karimoku, are continuing to invite well-known names to create new designs using Japanese techniques, keeping the theme of collaboration alive for another day. It's a clever marketing technique that gets Japanese design out into the world with a little helping hand from its Scandi allies.

The question is, why now? What is it about Japandi that so appeals today? The answer may be twofold. Firstly, it's true that the apparent serenity of Japan and Scandinavian culture appeals at this point in time. Our current existence is particularly chaotic and confusing for so many, and in times of discord we seek refuge. Japan and Scandinavia's quiet, humble way of being in the world is expressed in interiors that are plain, simple, and unoffensive. Collectively we are seeking comfort, and where better to find that sanctuary than in the domestic home, if you are so lucky to be able to. But secondly, as we become more concerned with the state of our planet, the concept of Japandi puts forward a more conscious way of living that rejects mass consumerism and materialism. It's a lifestyle that people have been living for centuries, but is something that we need to rediscover if we are to thrive. Japandi illustrates how design shouldn't necessarily be about the grand gestures, but the little positive changes you can make in the everyday.

This book aims to illustrate the enduring commonalities between Japanese and Scandinavian design, imparting lessons and learnings so that you can not only fall in love with the Japandi aesthetic and re-create the same look in your own home, but live and breathe the Japandi lifestyle too.

WHAT IS JAPANDI?

The term "Japandi" is a catchy portmanteau that is used to describe the close aesthetic connection between Japanese minimalism and Scandinavian design. The word marries these two complementary approaches into one recognizable interior style, but the concept of Japandi goes far beyond the look of a home.

From first glance, the Japandi aesthetic can be clearly defined by the use of natural materials, organic shapes, neutral tones, and clean lines. A Japandi interior is harmonious and manages to be both soothing in its uncluttered simplicity yet inviting in its rustic tactility. With Japandi, you get the Zen tranquility and refined order of Japanese interiors balanced with cozy Scandinavian style.

But Japandi isn't just about combining one element from Scandinavian design and another from Japanese design and hoping they'll go together. It's about taking inspiration from the shared principles that underpin these two traditions—simplicity, truth, honesty, purpose, functionality, and longevity. The appeal of Japandi is really in the ways in which Japan and Scandinavia can teach us about living more mindfully in the world. Their core values center on living in harmony with one's surroundings and in balance with nature, encouraging us to focus on the things that matter, use only what is necessary, and find happiness in the little things. Once you dig a little deeper, you will find that Japandi is much more than first meets the eye.

The Essence of Japandi

The concept of Japandi has three fundamental tenets—simplicity, harmony, and balance—that all interlink and work together to create the sense of calm that Japanese and Scandinavian interiors are so renowned for. You can use these three words as a framework to not only design in the Japandi way but embrace the lifestyle too.

SIMPLICITY

Simplicity celebrates the stillness and quiet that can come from anything that is plain, unobtrusive, or uncomplicated in nature. A simple lifestyle often means slowing down and curating your life or home with intention so there are fewer distractions. In Japandi terms, it is the idea of living with less and in turn freeing up space in the mind. The art of simplicity might come from the refined shape of a beautiful piece of handcrafted furniture or a pared-back color palette, but it can also be found in the celebration of little everyday moments and the practice of mindfulness. You can seek out simplicity in all aspects of your life, whether it is with your shopping habits, your surroundings, or from within yourself.

HARMONY

The dictionary describes harmony as a combination of parts that come together into a pleasing or orderly whole. For a Japandi interior this can mean that every design choice you make is united in telling the same story, so you create a cohesive, seamless feel where no object is fighting with another. You can

build harmony by using similar tones and textures, repeating certain elements throughout a space, or connecting inside and out. If we look at the bigger picture, the Japandi lifestyle also inspires a more harmonious way of being in the world, where nature is respected and cherished. This is reflected in the preference for natural materials, local craftsmanship, and the handmade.

BALANCE

Just like the idea of harmony, balance also expresses a state of peace where everything is in equilibrium or stability. The Japandi lifestyle encourages a feeling of balance with the outside world, within society, and within ourselves. As such, it places value on doing things in moderation or decorating with restraint.

A Japandi interior takes inspiration from nature and uses balanced asymmetry to prevent a space from feeling too contrived or staid. Instead there is a naturalness and feeling of life and movement, whether that's through the addition of a plant or the use of organic forms. Emotional balance is important too—neutral tones, simple furniture, and clutter-free rooms all combine to create a feeling of calm.

Scandinavian Design and the Japanese Aesthetic

In order to define the concept of Japandi, we first have to understand the individual worlds of Japanese and Scandinavian design, and how they compare with one another. They share some remarkable similarities in their design principles, but some key differences set them apart.

First, let's take the Scandinavian design tradition, which unites Denmark, Finland, Norway, and Sweden in one style (even if, technically, Finland isn't considered part of the geographical area of Scandinavia, which itself is a subset of the wider Nordic countries). Scandinavian style is seen as a timeless aesthetic that balances functional minimalism with a sense of coziness. Think of a Scandi interior, and you might picture a simple, clutter-free space with pared-back furnishings, light colors, and exposed wooden floors. There is typically an emphasis on clean lines, plain details, and plenty of natural light. Scandinavian homes may be clean and minimal, but there's also comfort and warmth from natural materials and organic elements, lending a relaxed, easygoing atmosphere to a space.

Most of all, Scandinavian interiors are understated—indulgence doesn't come from ostentation or spending a lot of money, but from doing a few things well, with longevity or quality in mind. This considered approach really encapsulates the Nordic values of equality, fairness, and democratic design.

In the Nordic countries, good design has always been seen as a way to improve the everyday lives of all, not just an elite few. Scandinavian design really came into its own in the early to mid-20th century, when designers such as Arne Jacobsen, Alvar Aalto, Hans J. Wegner, and Finn Juhl found international popularity with sculptural wooden furniture designs that were both functional and beautiful, cementing a visual language that has stuck to this day. Coming out of the Second World War, designers used their understanding of classic craftsmanship to

experiment with new techniques, pushing design innovation forward into a new world which rejected the shackles of the past.

Japanese design shares the simplicity of Scandinavian aesthetics but in a slightly different sense. It can also be seen as a form of minimalism that values functionality, but it tends to take it one step further with a more rigorous approach that is all about honesty, emptiness, and refinement. According to *The Essential Japanese House* by Teiji Itoh, it was considered vulgar to try to create any sense of beauty by adding ornamentation. Beauty instead was found in quiet restraint and moderation, often using only what was necessary and available. Japanese interiors are typically dominated by grid-like straight lines, rectilinear shapes, plain surfaces, wood, neutral colors, and low-lying furniture. Within this structured spatial framework, which traditionally tended to be designed around a modular unit that dictated the size of key features such as tatami mats, *fusuma* sliding doors, and *shoji* screens, there is space for natural asymmetry and textured materials to add warmth. A strong connection between inside and outside also gives life to Japanese-style spaces.

While Japanese interiors appear to have a certain level of perfectionism to them—even if they do seek out moments of material imperfection and irregular

THE BASIC PRINCIPLES OF SCANDINAVIAN DESIGN

Simplicity
A less-is-more approach that reduces things down without the need for superfluous details.

Functionality
The user is put first so that form and function work in harmony to create useful objects that can be enjoyed every day.

Democratic design
The designer's ego is eclipsed in favor of good-quality design that should be available to all, improving the lives of many, not just the few.

High-quality craftsmanship
A respect for the design heritage of the past and the creation of objects and spaces that are made to last.

Respect for nature
A deep-rooted appreciation of nature informs not only shapes, forms, and colors but inspires a more symbiotic relationship with the environment.

SEVEN PRINCIPLES OF JAPANESE AESTHETICS

Kanso (simplicity)
The elimination of anything that is unnecessary, including clutter, with the aim of complete clarity and purity.

Datsuzoku (freedom from habit or routine)
Seeking beauty in the unconventional and ethereal to create moments that take you away from the ordinary.

Fukinsei (asymmetry)
A desire to convey the irregularity and asymmetry found in the natural world.

Seijaku (tranquility)
A state of serenity and stillness that helps quieten the mind.

Shibui (understated)
A simple, unobtrusive beauty that is humble and without ornamentation.

Yūgen (profound grace)
A suggestion or sense of openness that invites a mysterious sense of wonder about the world that is hard to put into words.

Shizen (naturalness)
Re-creating a resemblance of nature and avoiding anything that is artificial or fake.

naturalness here and there—there is also a poetic element to their approach that separates them from Scandinavian design. The particular Zen quality of Japanese spaces comes from the perfect balance between logic and emotion. With spiritual origins in Zen Buddhism and the nature religion of Shintoism, the Japanese minimalism we see today has a symbolism to it that proves sometimes hard to define in Western terms. In 1971, the Zen Buddhist philosopher Hisamatsu Shin'ichi identified seven principles that defined Japanese aesthetics, influencing everything from Zen gardens to ceramics and design. These are *kanso* (simplicity), *fukinsei* (asymmetry), *shibui* (understated), *shizen* (naturalness), *datsuzoku* (freedom from habit or routine), *seijaku* (tranquility), and *yūgen* (profound grace). They are all qualities that define nature, as well as ideal human virtues, and together they work in harmony to create the elusive concept of *wabi sabi*. There are many subtleties to Japanese design but these principles help describe the poised stillness found in Japanese interiors, where nothing is left to chance but everything comes together to create a feeling of awe in the simple and natural.

Of course, Scandinavian and Japanese interiors can vary greatly, and you can have both bold, colorful Scandi-style spaces as well as neutral spaces, and very intricate Japanese spaces in addition to stark, minimalist spaces. As Scandinavian style describes four separate countries, it's hard to put them all in one box; there are slight variations between each of their styles, influenced by their own unique design histories and cultures. And while there may be a particular vision of Japanese interiors in the West, that doesn't always tell the full story or adequately represent the wide range of diversity that can be found in the different regions across Japan. To that extent, Japanese and Scandinavian design shouldn't be seen as trends of the moment, but two complex aesthetic traditions with a rich heritage that gives them both depth and meaning.

Nordic and Japanese Philosophies

Japandi style can't be discussed without referring to a number of Nordic and Japanese lifestyle philosophies that have found their way into modern parlance. There are the Japanese concepts of *wabi sabi*, which seeks out beauty in imperfection and impermanence, and *ikigai*, which centers around the idea of finding one's sense of purpose. Combine those with the Danish and Norwegian idea of hygge, which is about fostering a feeling of coziness and connection, and the Swedish term *lagom*, which encourages us to enjoy life in moderation, and you have the essence of Japandi.

There must be a reason why the Nordic countries consistently rank as some of the happiest nations, or why Japan has one of the longest life expectancies in the world. While a healthy lifestyle and plenty of time spent outside might play a role, the likely answer probably has more to do with the dedicated pursuit of a life lived with more purpose, presence, and intention. The idea of hygge is perhaps one of Scandinavia's biggest cultural exports, finding universal popularity recently as people sought to bring more comfort into their chaotic lives with a simple moment of self-care. It seems we all want a taste of Nordic contentment.

Hygge, *wabi sabi, ikigai*, and *lagom* seem to have become something of a new religion for a world that has lost its way. In the West, people tend to be obsessed with improvement and perfecting everything from our bodies to our Instagram feeds. We're always so busy trying to optimize every moment that we forget to enjoy the present. But these lifestyle concepts teach us how to slow down and live in the moment, find purpose in everyday life, and celebrate the quieter joys that give us a reason for being.

WABI SABI

Like many of these lifestyle philosophies, the ancient Japanese concept of *wabi sabi* proves ambiguous and hard to translate directly into English. In its simplest terms, it can be described as an aesthetic ideal that seeks out beauty in imperfection. Often misunderstood, in recent years it has been adopted by the West and dumbed down to become the embodiment of a certain type of rustic interior. But with roots in Zen Buddhism, *wabi sabi* is so much more than a look or style. There's an emotional quality to it too. *Wabi sabi* should in fact be seen as a way of thinking that accepts the ephemerality of life and the transience of nature—the idea that everything is inherently flawed or in flux, and nothing really lasts forever. It's a concept the Japanese had to learn the hard way, living with the unpredictability of earthquakes, typhoons, and tsunamis.

Wabi and *sabi* were originally seen as two separate ideas with slightly different meanings, but over time they have become intertwined as one. In Japanese aesthetics, *wabi* was first used to convey a feeling of loneliness or solitude in nature, while *sabi* referred to a sense of desolation. That might all sound a bit melancholy, but Zen monks believed that if they could free themselves from the bounds of the material world and live in pure simplicity, it would result in mental enlightenment. They saw a hidden beauty in the modest and humble, or even the ugly and unrefined. Later *wabi sabi* found its greatest expression in the traditional Japanese tearoom, with its cracked earth walls and simple setting.

Today *wabi sabi* translates as an unpretentious aesthetic that celebrates the patina of time with weathered materials and raw textures. It is the opposite of ostentation, grandeur, or splendor. Instead, it is quiet and inward looking, preferring subdued lighting, muted colors, and layers of intimacy. Wear and tear is actively celebrated and sought out. As Irene Chang from Maana Homes says (see interview, pages 84–87), "To me, *wabi sabi* is really a lifelong practice. As a designer, you have to let go of the idea of perfection, but also embracing imperfection is a whole other level. To really truly understand that you have to take a step back, and just allow something to be the way it is and constantly remind yourself that's what makes it beautiful."

IKIGAI

Ikigai is a Japanese concept that translates simply as "a reason for being." It's what gives you a sense of purpose and makes your life worth living; the fuel that feeds your soul and drives you forward each day. As the French would say, it's your *raison d'être*. For Erin Niimi Longhurst, author of *Japonisme*, your *ikigai* is something that is rarely straightforward or immediately obvious: "It's slowly revealed to you over time, in the moments that help you to get to know yourself. It's never complete, and is constantly in flux." Finding a sense of fulfillment in life might not necessarily come from just one thing either; you might find your *ikigai* from connections in your social life or from a satisfying week at work or a moment you take out of the day for yourself. True *ikigai* converges on the balance of four principles: your passion, your mission, your profession, and your vocation. It's about understanding what you're good at and what value you can bring to the world.

HYGGE

With Danish and Norwegian origins, hygge (pronounced *hoo-ga*) has become a common expression in the interiors world, and even beyond—so much so it was added to the *Oxford English Dictionary* in 2017. Many people want to adopt the Scandinavian feeling of coziness that comes with this cultural phenomena. But ask a Danish person how they would describe hygge and they will say it's more than just candlelight and blankets. It's not just a word they use to define a cozy moment—where something might be described as *hyggelig*—it's also part of their cultural identity and an expression of the healthy work/life balance they strive for, where value is placed on taking time out of your routine to enjoy simple pleasures. In that sense, it's a state of mind that encourages you to slow down and be more present. This seems somewhat in contrast to the Western lifestyle of chasing a dream, always working hard, and finding little time for vacations or moments of escapism.

Hygge is therefore also a feeling of close connection, kinship, and togetherness, whether that's with yourself or with others. The word has been variously attributed to the Old Norse word *hyggja*, meaning "to think," as well as *hugr*, meaning "hug" or "mood." It was really a way for the Scandinavians to get through the harsh, freezing winters and seek out warmth and comfort. Today, moments of hygge aren't just found in fall and winter, it's a concept that works in any season. A relaxed picnic in the summer sunshine can be considered hygge, as can spending time in nature or sharing a heartwarming home-cooked meal. In the home, hygge can be expressed with cozy textures, warm materials, and inviting focal points, such as a window seat or fireplace. But it's also about what you do in the home and creating opportunities to unwind or uplift the soul.

LAGOM

Lagom is a Swedish term that can be translated as "just enough" or the balance between "not too much, not too little." Rather than restricting yourself or taking things away from your life, it's more about having the ideal quantity of something, or in other words, enjoying less, but better. As the Swedish proverb *lagom är bäst* says, "The right amount is best." It reflects the very Scandinavian values of modesty and equality, where it would appear vulgar to take too much or show off your extravagance or flashiness. Likewise in Japan, it's not seen as socially acceptable to stand out and be boastful. Living a *lagom* lifestyle also means being respectful of the environment and paying attention to the resources you're using. In the home, it might mean that you have just enough for what you need or that you prioritize reusing certain items and recycling what you no longer want. The Finnish have a similar word, *sopivasti*, which means "just right," while the Norwegian term *passe* can be used to describe something that is adequate, suitable, or in balance.

The Simple Everyday

The idea of enjoying the little things in life is central to Japandi. It's not just about taking the time to curate a beautiful home, but also making the effort to be more present and intentional across all aspects of life. Japandi rejects a fast pace in favor of the celebration of simple everyday moments.

Often it is the small joys that add up to a more fulfilling life as a whole. To understand that, we have to reconnect with ourselves. In the home, that means becoming more aware of our environment, rather than just passing through it in the rush of our routines. In our busy schedules, we can be guilty of missing the tiny nuances of everyday life, whether that's the feel of the sun on our skin, the way the light dances through a window, or the ritual of enjoying our first cup of coffee of the day. The concept of Japandi encourages us to draw comfort and inspiration from the seemingly ordinary.

Perfection in this context is seen as counterproductive, unnatural, and ultimately unattainable, especially when we're talking about real homes that see their fair share of wear and tear. *Wabi sabi* can help us fall back in love with our homes, with all their flaws and imperfections. Often when we're living in a space day-to-day we focus on all the faults and things we want to change, but someone stepping into the space for the first time will likely only see the beauty and best bits. *Lagom* also encourages us to make do and rediscover possessions that we might have previously overlooked. The Japandi aesthetic is about appreciating that things are rarely perfect, and often the idealized versions of things aren't what truly makes us happy. Homes should be lived in and loved. There might be a ring mark on the table, mismatched ceramics, a scuffed stool in the corner, or cracked vase on a shelf, but that's okay and even desirable.

The Rise of Japandi

AN INTERVIEW WITH JEREMY SMART

Based in Tokyo, Jeremy Smart is the co-editor in chief of *Design Anthology*, a media brand and biannual print magazine dedicated to documenting the creative culture across Asia Pacific. Jeremy is also a creative director, brand strategist, and commentator on design, having written for newspaper *Nikkei Asia* and worked with the likes of MUJI, Aesop, Louis Vuitton, and Rosewood Hotels. Here he offers a unique insight into the world of Japanese design today.

Why do you think that Japandi is having a moment right now?

Japanese design has an enduring appeal but I think it probably speaks more to where Japan is at the moment. Japan is finding its voice again; it's got this newfound confidence that maybe it didn't have up until the Covid-19 pandemic. There was a long period where Japan was being sidelined, or sidelining itself, from a lot of conversations that were geopolitical and to do with its relationship with other countries, on both a government and business level. Japan has been domestically inward-looking for a really long time and it feels like that's changed now, in so many different areas. As Japanese companies are looking overseas for growth, these collaborations are as much a marketing exercise as they are creative endeavors.

The way people access Japanese design is so much easier now, and I think people are really curious and want to go deeper in their experiences too. Tourists come here and they're interested in actually visiting factories or craftspeople and seeing things being made, rather than just viewing them in a retail setting or museum. Sometimes I meet people who don't live here but they have such a knowledge and interest around Japanese design that it's almost like it's an obsession.

Do you think that the Zen quality of Japanese design also appeals?

Even at a commercial level, Japan is now seen as somewhere that's safe, secure, and predictable. Japanese interiors also reflect that, where spaces have become a refuge from disruption. Japan had this narrative of a declining population but now, in comparison to the rest of the world, it appears comfortably predictable and that can be really appealing. In a chaotic world, people seek security, so in a lot of ways, interiors are really quiet demonstrations of a global mood.

Living in Japan, do you see the influence of Scandinavian design?

I think there's a lot of innate similarities between Japanese and Scandinavian design, but it doesn't feel like a trend here. To a certain degree, there probably always has been a natural synergy. But when you talk to the designers, that is what they are inspired by. If you look at design fairs as a snapshot of that, that's where the excitement and the hunger is, not just for inspiration, but for partnership.

Do you think the concept of *wabi sabi* is still alive in Japan today?

I can't say that it's a phrase that ever comes up in conversation here, which I think maybe says something. We know what *wabi sabi* looks like in English—it's become a symbol of an aesthetic style—whereas in Japanese I think there's a lot more meaning and nuance to it.

There's also a bit of a paradox between the high and low in Japan. If a new apartment building goes up here, it's quite important that things do not visibly age, which kind of flies in the face of what you might expect. There's a real respect for nature and natural materials here, but it does seem like the average consumer wants this kind of eternal newness, and spaces are designed accordingly.

How would you describe Japanese design today?

It's simple and functional, but spaces are designed for the senses and have this warm, tactile quality. There's a national obsession with nature, not just in a literal sense, but in an emotional, spiritual sense, and often it isn't about the material itself but the ideas behind it. Wood, for example, is so deeply rooted in Japanese design. There's a consciousness of what nature is doing at any given point.

Then with the idea of simple functionalism, there's just this obsession with fixing every problem. I think the desire to polish the edges of society and the world around us is unique to Japan. Such care goes into every product. There's a real calmness to living here and it's absolutely addictive, because of the way people are. People tend to be so fixated on the big milestones of life, but actually life is what's happening every day, so if you fix those small everyday things, it can have the biggest impact on your quality of life.

I think it's ironic because we're talking about an aesthetic that's become a trend, but ironically both design cultures are probably the least obsessed with aesthetics. They're so focused on functionality and doing things properly that the calm, minimal aesthetic is just a natural outcome of those values. I like that it comes from just making spaces people want to be in, and that feel good to be in.

Craft in Japan

AN INTERVIEW WITH KYLIE CLARK

Passionate about all things Japanese, Kylie Clark is a Japan specialist consultant who has more than twenty years' experience working for Japanese government agencies across the travel, art, craft, design, and food and drinks industries. She was previously director of PR and communications at Japan House London, as well as head of experiences at Pantechnicon, a cultural hub of Nordic and Japanese design in London's Belgravia. Here she offers her insight into Japanese design.

Why do you think people are intrigued by Japanese design at the moment?

I think it ties into a greater awareness of environmental issues. Japanese design focuses on things that are simple, well made, good quality, and don't tend to date; the type of things that will become more beautiful the more you use them. There have been so many reports of consumers buying tableware, only for it to be thrown away after one season, just like fast fashion, and that's not how things should be consumed. I think that the more minimalist style of Japanese design is really timeless. You see pieces of Japanese ceramics that are hundreds of years old but they look like the sort of things that are completely on trend now.

Do you think the concept of *wabi sabi* is still alive in Japan today?

I think it's a concept that has been interpreted by the West in a way that is easy to understand, which isn't a bad thing, but it is thought of differently in Japan. *Wabi sabi* is often not just the asymmetrical or imperfect, it's also the old, worn patina that comes from something being used a lot. One of the things that keeps me constantly fascinated by Japan is that the more that you know about the country and the more that you learn about Japanese aesthetics, the more you realize you don't know. There are so many layers of meaning in a painting or piece of ceramic or an interior, and even if something looks simple or natural, there's usually a lot of depth and thought behind it. And often within Japanese culture a lot is not said and assumed as knowledge. I first lived in Japan when I was sixteen and discovered there's lots of nuanced meanings to every aspect of Japanese society.

Do you think that the Zen quality of Japanese design also appeals?

A beautiful piece of Japanese art or craft work definitely has a calming influence. In Japan, there's a different way of thinking, where things don't have to be perfectly symmetrical, because nature's not. One thing that's really popular in Japan is single-stem vases. Often you only need to appreciate one flower and that can be seen as more tranquil for the mind.

What do you think are the biggest misconceptions of Japanese design?

Japan is not just one aesthetic and it's a common misconception that Japanese design is only minimalist in style. It's true that the dominant aesthetic is very simple but there are many aspects of Japanese design that are extremely intricate, such as Imari porcelain. Japan has a huge number of hoarders and people who have lots of things in their house too.

In contrast to Scandinavian design, Japanese design seems to be more cautious of change, do you think that's true?

In recent years the word innovate is heard often in any debate about the future of Japanese craft. It's become widely accepted in Japan that craft needs to adapt and be relevant to modern lifestyles to survive. So change is happening, but perhaps at a slower pace than in the Nordics. Within Japanese craft, there tends to be very distinct styles in different parts of the country. A certain area might have a particular type of craft that is done in a certain way and it can be very hard to do something different. I think this rigidity comes from the fact that in Japan, people tend to strive to protect whatever they're doing. They will learn from a master who has spent years perfecting their craft and there's so much respect for them that it is then quite hard to go your own way. This may be why there has been a growing trend of Japanese craftspeople collaborating with European designers to develop new products.

In both Scandinavian and Japanese cultures, design is seen as democratic and part of the everyday experience. Do you agree?

Yes, in Japan, design is simply part of everyday life. For example, most families in Japan will have beautiful pieces that have been handed down through the generations. Tableware in Japanese households tends to be mismatching—each family member will have their own rice bowl, miso soup bowl, chopsticks, and teacup that they have chosen depending on their personality. They're all so simple and classic that it all goes together beautifully on the table. It doesn't matter if it's mismatched; that's what makes it beautiful.

What do you think is the biggest takeaway that we can learn from Japanese design?

If we could think of things as lasting for many many years, so instead of buying something on a whim, we see the investment of how long we'll be using it and the pleasure it will give us. For example, having a beautiful cup to drink your tea from every morning makes such a difference. If we value things and become more conscious consumers, we can also help support independent makers. Craft in Japan is struggling to find young people to carry on the skills and traditions. It is a dying art and it makes a huge impact on Japanese craftspeople when non-Japanese people buy their work. There is a very active movement in Japan to try and get publicity and appreciation of Japanese craft overseas so that more young people will be interested in taking up those sorts of jobs.

We can also take the time to appreciate what we've got, do you think?

In Japan everything is reused and rarely are things flippantly thrown away. That's seen with things like *kintsugi*, the fixing of broken ceramics, or *sashiko*, the mending of textiles with beautiful stitching techniques. There are now kits you can get to do these things at home and the result can be absolutely stunning. Hopefully now we're on the tip of a whole change in thinking about how we consume.

WELL-BEING
IN THE HOME

Design for well-being is concerned with how we perceive and experience spaces. It's a holistic approach that considers the emotional quality of an interior and how our surroundings make us feel. Because our homes are not just places to keep us warm and dry, they're also spaces that can provide a sense of comfort and connection. When designed well, they have the power to nurture, inspire, and help us flourish.

Well-being can generally be described as a state of contentment and good health. When we're stressed or overwhelmed by the world, we tend to seek relief and refuge in our interior spaces. Our homes often act as sanctuaries, where we can escape to unplug and unwind amongst the chaos of everyday life.

But we first have to understand what brings us peace and calm. A Japandi-style home listens to its owners; it never shouts over them. The user is always put first. Designing for well-being is an introspective process that forces us to take a closer look at what we need from a space, not just practically, but emotionally too. You might feel soothed by the touch of soft textures, uplifted by a green view, or calmed by the sight of a clutter-free space with everything in its place. You could find you need a contemplative corner to retreat to, a window seat to focus your wandering mind, or a cocoon-like bedroom to get a good night's sleep. These are the things that will give a home purpose and meaning.

A Mindful Approach

The Japanese and Scandinavians share an approach to design that is very intentional. Every element is carefully considered and reflected on in a slow, thoughtful way. The aim is always to create a space with built-in longevity; somewhere that can evolve and endure long after the design has been "finished" and finalized.

Some people might think that minimalism is about taking things away and depriving yourself of any joy or color. But in reality, it's actually an approach that can help you get more from your interior, though not in the obvious ways you might think. The simplicity and contemplative stillness that comes from a Japandi-style space often opens up more possibilities for what really matters in life.

It can be said that the Japanese and Scandinavians are proponents of slow living. This is a lifestyle choice that encourages a more conscious way of viewing and appreciating the world, and the part we play in it. As the name suggests, it's also about slowing down and savoring what we have. Slow living rejects convenience, mass production, and a fast-paced, throwaway lifestyle in favor of mindful decisions and intentional habits. It's mending an old sweater, cooking from scratch using seasonal produce, or putting your phone away and spending time in nature.

When it comes to creating a home, slow design is about being mindful of the things we put into our interiors. It is designing not according to trends or what someone says is hot, or not, but because something appeals to us on a deeper level. To do that, we have to first understand the different layers that go into making a home.

KEY PRINCIPLES OF DESIGNING A JAPANDI HOME

A mindful home

The Japandi approach is all about taking a more thoughtful, introspective view of design and decorating, so as to create spaces that stand the test of time. Take a moment to think about what your home can offer and how you will be using the space every day. For a home to be a true reflection of who you are and what you need, you have to better understand yourself first. Think about interior design as a bit like therapy for the home. Consider what brings you joy and what kind of spaces you're better suited to. Do you need to factor in lots of storage to hide away clutter? Would you like a reading nook for all your books? Do you practice yoga and need a flexible space to move about in?

Find meaning

Make a list of all the functions and daily moments you need to account for, then think about how each room should feel when you walk through the door. If you find yourself looking for inspiration, whether online or in magazines, try to really analyze what it is about that particular image that appeals to you. Break it down and look for the intention behind the design. For example, do you like that color because it reminds you of something? Are you drawn to that material texture because it evokes a certain feeling? If you make sure there is a reason behind every element in your home, rather than just copying what you've seen, it will create a more honest, authentic space.

Define your values

In order to find your purpose or as the Japanese would say, your *ikigai* (your reason for being), you need to first understand your core values. Your values will shape your interior choices and be expressed in your surroundings. Ideally there should be a harmony between who you are and what your home says about you. To begin with, it can help to pick out three words that describe the home you want to create. This gives you a framework to guide you through the design process, so if you start to veer off track you can always come back to your three words and check if something aligns with your values. Your three-word mantra could be, for example, "simple, honest, and sustainable" or "classic, elegant, and refined."

Simplicity

The key to Japanese and Scandinavian design is knowing when to stop. Simplicity allows for a sense of openness, in more meanings than one. It creates a restful feeling and space for objects to breathe, but it also allows everyday life to take center stage, so a space comes to life with use rather than more "stuff." In his book *Just Enough Design*, graphic designer Taku Satoh describes *hodo-hodo* as design that deliberately holds back, leaving room for users to engage with objects or spaces as they see fit. *Hodo-hodo* can be translated as "leave well enough alone." When a design shows restraint, Satoh says, "it serves as a nearly limitless canvas for self-expression." Simplicity is only including what is truly necessary. It might mean taking one thing away from a composition before it can be considered complete.

Tactility and textures

Touch is so important when it comes to designing a home—we should feel comfortable and as though we're able to properly relax. Japandi interiors embrace texture and tend to complement simplicity with the raw, rustic, and cozy. Once you have a clear vision for your space, turn away from the screens and gather some material or fabric samples to create a physical mood board. A considered material palette will help you balance textures and create moments of tactility. Do they feel warm and soft to touch? Have you balanced the hard and rough with the smooth and delicate?

Natural inspiration

The addition of nature in an interior space is proven to reduce stress and boost our mood. Japandi interiors are a good example of how we can bring the outside in and design spaces that use more natural elements. As humans we tend to have a preference toward the natural over the synthetic or artificial, so as well as adding plants and considering views of nature, make sure to prioritize natural materials, textures, and motifs.

Design to last

Japanese and Scandinavian design are both inherently mindful of the impact we have on the environment. Think carefully about the design choices you're making, and consider where something has come from, how it's been made, and by whom, and whether you could find something similar secondhand.

Calm and coziness

Japandi spaces have a quiet beauty that brings focus to life's simple moments. Interiors are designed according to function, but there's still room for comfort and coziness. Consider injecting your life with some Japandi-inspired daily rituals to help you slow down and appreciate your surroundings. For example, create a tea or coffee station with your favorite ceramics where you can spend a mindful moment taking a break, curate a focal point on a sideboard with a sculptural floral arrangement, or simply enjoy the moment at the end of the day when you can light the candles and relax. Start as you mean to go on and set the foundations for a restorative, clutter-free space that makes you feel good, not stressed.

Design for the Senses

We don't just use our eyes to experience a space. We rely on all our senses to understand and relate to our surroundings. Touch helps ground and calm us, scent can evoke strong memories, and sound might stir up emotions. With this in mind, Japandi interiors are designed to offer a complete sensory experience.

By paring things back aesthetically and practicing restraint, Japandi design draws a heightened awareness to all senses. The focus of our experience shifts then from the purely visual to the haptic, bringing attention to the little details—the tactility of materials, the way the light falls, or how we move through space. A Japandi interior allows room for each sense, so that the experience of that space becomes meditative and purposeful. Our eye might be drawn to a single branch in a vase, or a view through one room to another; our heart rate might be soothed by subdued sounds that are softened by sound-insulating textiles; or we might be enveloped by the scent of natural materials and be transported for a moment into nature.

These moments are what give the Japandi style a compelling, emotional quality. The Japanese are particularly spiritual in this approach. Japanese Zen masters believed that spiritual freedom and contentment could be found by detaching from material things and observing lessons from nature. Without the need for spectacle or flamboyance, they relied on the senses to give interior spaces meaning and intrigue. The beauty of Japandi interiors is therefore often in the overlooked moments and hidden details. If we slow down and focus on the whole experience of a space, we can create a home that better supports our whole well-being.

HOW TO DESIGN FOR THE SENSES

Sight

Create small, focused pockets of detail in a room that the eye can focus on. Consider viewpoints and use furniture and artwork to construct inviting focal areas. There should be free, negative space between these points of interest so that the eye isn't overwhelmed by too many things. For example, if you have shelves either side of a chimney breast with beautiful objects on display, leave the chimney breast bare so it doesn't look too crowded. Thinks about creating an element of surprise here and there, so a room doesn't reveal all its visual tricks at once. It makes for a more compelling home if there is a process of discovery, such as a beautiful pendant light leading you up the stairs or a well-curated sideboard at the end of a hallway, inviting you to see what lives beyond.

Sound

Calm comes from a tranquil environment undisturbed by loud sounds. If you live in a busy urban area or have close neighbors, find ways to try and block out noise from the outside world to protect your peace. Rugs, soft furnishings, acoustic wall panels, cork, or wooden walls and curtains all help absorb sounds.

Touch

Touch is one of the most important senses for our well-being as it is how we first learned to experience the world. Through touch we can understand the temperature of something or how safe or dangerous an object is. Tactility is what will give a home comfort. We can appeal to our sense of touch with rich textures and natural materials, choosing soft edges over hard corners and warm surfaces instead of cold finishes. Don't forget the touch points in a space—the door handles, light switches, cabinet pulls, and plug sockets—it's the little details that make all the difference.

Smell

Scent can be powerfully evocative, transporting us to certain places or memories. You can add fragrance with fresh flowers, naturally scented candles, incense, and oil burners, but you should also think about the materials you use in a space. Try to avoid paint or man-made materials that are high in toxic volatile organic compounds (VOCs). VOCs are the airborne chemicals that are released by a surface into the atmosphere.

Vestibular

This is our sense of balance, which helps with our orientation in a space. To create a more comfortable environment, pay attention to uneven surfaces or visual illusions that could make a space feel disorientating, such as patterned floor tiles. Avoid shiny, reflective surfaces that could have a dizzying effect.

Proprioception (or spatial awareness)

This is the awareness we have of our body in space. It's how we can walk without thinking about the next step or easily move up stairs. Make sure there's enough room to get past furniture and consider the scale of objects next to each other. For example, it might feel uncomfortable if you had to reach down from a bed to a low bedside table. Make sure that a space is intuitive to use, so you don't even have to think about it.

The Art of Simplicity

Simplicity is design in moderation. It is the sense of purity and harmony that comes from a lack of decoration and unnecessary complication. In a Japandi interior it is expressed with muted neutral colors, reductionist forms, and minimal, if any, ornamentation or detail. Like minimalism, it can be considered a lifestyle choice, describing an approach that emphasizes having fewer possessions and less clutter. In Japanese design, the art of simplicity is known as *kanso*, and is considered one of the foundations of the *wabi sabi* philosophy.

The concept of simplicity can be found both in Japanese design and Scandinavian interiors. In the West, simplicity came out of modernism and the Bauhaus movement as a rejection of the ornamentation of the past. With the motto "form follows function," the emphasis was placed on functional designs and simplified forms that could be mass-produced. Today, the Scandinavian aesthetic can be defined by clean lines, the economical use of materials, and simple, light-filled spaces. Japanese architect Kenya Hara makes the observation in the book *WA: The Essence of Japanese Design*, that while simplicity in the West was based on rationality, the simplicity of the Japanese aesthetic can better be described as a form of "emptiness." The idea is to use as little design as possible, leaving a sense of openness or space that can be interpreted by the user. That emptiness can be found in everything from the bare space of the traditional tea house to the minimalist, anonymous packaging of everyday objects from stores like MUJI. In this way, simplicity is less formal and defined by rules, and more poetical in meaning. It acts more like stillness or silence, a pregnant pause waiting for possibilities to unfold.

Kanso is one of the seven principles of Japanese aesthetics that define the *wabi sabi* philosophy (see page 22). *Kanso* means paring things back and editing out anything that is superfluous. *Kanso* creates room for *ma*, or negative space, which is valued as much as positive space or the precise placement of objects or art. The thinking is that when a space is curated with just the bare essentials, focus is drawn to specific elements in a room and they take on an even greater sense of beauty. *Kanso* can also be described as the state of mind that results from a life of simplicity, creating a feeling of inner peace and quiet. In his book *Wabi-Sabi for Artists, Designers, Poets & Philosophers*, Leonard Koren says simplicity is best described as "the state of grace arrived at by a sober, modest, heartfelt intelligence." Japandi simplicity therefore inspires visual as well as physical and mental calm.

Less, but Better

A clutter-free space is key to the Zen-like quality of a Japandi-style home. There is a certain restraint that is practiced with the deliberate placement of select objects and furniture, and any unsightly things are carefully hidden away out of view. Not only does decluttering lend focus and order to a space, the act of letting go can also be a calming and cathartic process that will help you fall back in love with your home.

Clutter can easily make us feel overwhelmed and helpless—you only need to think of the tangle of wires in the corner, the overflowing cutlery drawer, or the closet door you can't quite shut, and you can begin to feel the visual and metaphorical weight of your baggage. Realistically, we don't need twenty different mugs or ten sets of the same white bedding, but it's easy for things to accumulate and get on top of you. In a materialistic society that is constantly chasing more, the act of decluttering helps teach us about the emotional value of objects. Instead of holding on to things just for the sake of it, or treating objects as disposable and infinitely replaceable, decluttering helps highlight the meaning that objects give to your life. This way of understanding objects through our relationship with them is a very Japanese approach. The objects you do then have out on display carry a greater weight because they've been chosen to fulfill a purpose or because they connect with you on a deeply personal level.

It was Japanese organization specialist Marie Kondo who really popularized the emotional potential of decluttering in 2011 with her bestselling book *The Life-Changing Magic of Tidying Up*, setting off a worldwide obsession for packing cubes and folding T-shirts into satisfying squares. Her KonMari method encourages us to only hold on to the things that "spark joy," or *tokimeku* in Japanese. Items should be sorted one category at a time, before finding a

designated spot for each object—the idea being that it is then easier to keep a space tidy and organized.

For Kondo, decluttering is as much a mindset as a physical process—the act of tidying is used to better understand oneself and what you want from your home, and indeed life. Kondo references the inspiration of feng shui and the Japanese equivalent called *fusui*, which seeks to create a harmonious flow of energy in a space. The Chinese practice of feng shui has careful rules about the arrangement of furniture in order to create a better balance between yourself, your environment, and the natural world. The idea is that our homes are a reflection of our inner lives. If your home is cluttered and chaotic, it might symbolize an imbalance in your internal world. The key is to align the energy of your home with the essence of who you are.

Kondo's method also has roots in the ancient religion of Japan, Shintoism, which posits that there is an energy or divine spirit in all things, called *kami*. It could be described as the essence that makes an object unique. In Japanese culture, there is a link or bond between an owner and their object. This is why Kondo encourages people to thank discarded items before letting them go. It's paying respect to the part they played in your life. In the process, it opens up a renewed gratitude for our homes and the things we already have. This form of minimalism isn't necessarily about restriction, but surrounding yourself only with the things you really love.

Fumio Sasaki, on the other hand, is a more extreme purist, choosing to live in a tiny 320-square-foot (30-sq-m) room with just 150 possessions in total. His idea of minimalism, detailed in his 2017 book *Goodbye, Things*, centers on the Japanese art of *danshari,* a three-step decluttering process that encourages you to become more mindful of the things you bring into your home. *Dan* is the first step and is the act of refusing, by resisting consumerism and the temptation of impulse buys. It's about reframing what you really need and changing your shopping habits to suit. *Sha* means to dispose of and is the process of sorting through your things, while the final step, *ri*, is about separation and detaching yourself from your possessions.

Some of Sasaki's concepts stem from Zen Buddhism and the idea that we can find greater inner peace and contentment by letting go of our emotional attachment to material things. It was Buddha who said that attachment is the root of all suffering. Holding on to things can be our way of controlling our environment, but this doesn't always serve us in the long term or make us happy. Instead it can be freeing to understand that material things may come and go, but they are not what defines our value. By clearing the mental clutter as well as the physical clutter, and continuing to satisfy ourselves with enough, we can create space and freedom for the things that make us feel good. In that way it also links to *wabi* (as in one half of *wabi sabi*), which can be used to describe a simple, modest way of living in peaceful solitude from the material world.

Whether you take the KonMari or Danshari method, or something in between, editing your life down and choosing to live with less, but better, can bring peace of mind and help you reconnect with your home. In a world of excess, there are a lot of lessons that can be learned.

THE ART OF DECLUTTERING

Have a strategy
You're more likely to take action and stick to the act of decluttering if you have a clear plan. It might help to create a list of areas that need focus, then you can tick them off as you go.

Step by step
It can often be too overwhelming to think of your home as a whole and picture all the things that need to be sorted. Instead, break it down into accessible chunks, whether it's by room, by item, or even just one drawer at a time. Then create a manageable schedule, for example, a different room every weekend.

Change your mindset
Bring focus to the practice of decluttering by thinking about what you want to get out of it. Write down your goals and how you envisage feeling in the space afterward—this will motivate you to keep going. You can even go a bit deeper and start to think about what meaning you get from the things you have. Are you holding on to something because it's trendy?

Sort
When going through items, divide them into "keep," "chuck," and "maybe" piles. Anything in the chuck pile is to be sold or recycled, the keep pile is to be sorted and put back in place, and the maybe pile are things that deserve a second look. Try to be strong; if something's broken and you're unlikely to fix it, let it go.

Questions to ask yourself
During the sorting process, reflect on an object's value in your life. Ask yourself, How often do I use this? Have I used it in the last month? Or even six months? Do I have something similar? How does it make me feel when I look at it? Does it go with anything else I have? What is it that is making me hold onto it?

Let go
Practice the art of detachment and try to separate yourself from the story of the object. Take a moment to appreciate what that object gave to your life, understand why it isn't adding value to your life right now, then quickly move onto the next item.

A place for everything
The most satisfying part of decluttering is putting everything back where it's meant to be. Give surfaces and cupboards a good clean then use boxes, baskets, and trays to sort items so they're easy to find. You're more likely to keep on top of clutter if everything has a clear home.

Keep the habit going
Once you've had your initial big declutter, have regular tidy-up sessions. One handy trick is to have a basket for discarded objects and place one unwanted item in it every day, every week, or every month. You can then distribute to thrift stores, recycle, or sell as needed.

One in one out
If you're looking to control the things that come into your home, start a one-in-one-out policy. If you're buying a new item, you need to get rid of an old one first.

Soft Minimalism

AN INTERVIEW WITH JONAS BJERRE-POULSEN, FOUNDER OF NORM ARCHITECTS

Norm Architects is a Copenhagen-based architecture and design practice founded in 2008 by Jonas Bjerre-Poulsen and Kasper Rønn. Guided by the purpose of well-being, their human-centric approach to design can be described as "soft minimalism." Whether it's a pared-back retreat in the Swedish forest, a coastal home in a secluded corner of Denmark, or a luxury apartment in a quiet residential area of Tokyo, their projects celebrate tactility, craft tradition, and the beauty of natural materials. Having worked extensively in Japan, including with good friend and close collaborator Keiji Ashizawa (see interview, pages 156–159) for Japanese brand Karimoku, here Jonas Bjerre-Poulsen describes the aesthetic kinship that keeps drawing their practice to Japan.

What first drew you to Japanese aesthetics?

Growing up in suburban Denmark, we have been exposed to Japanese influences our whole lives. Throughout the 1960s and '70s, a vast number of houses were built with open floor plans and large floor-to-ceiling sliding doors opening onto a walled garden inside the house. The interior surfaces were made from warm, natural materials, with an extensive use of wood, and sculptural greens and bamboo in the garden. Even though I had no idea at that time, the connection to traditional Japanese architecture could clearly be sensed.

    Later during my studies, I was very interested in the relation between modernism and traditional Japanese architecture, particularly in relation to the works of Frank Lloyd Wright, Mies van der Rohe, and many others working in the US. So, from the beginning of Norm Architects, Japanese aesthetics has been a great source of inspiration, without us having ever visited the country. It was not until we attended a workshop less than a decade ago in southern Japan, with the brand Ariake, that we experienced Japan for the first time, and we have been hooked ever since. It is a strange feeling of aesthetic kinship that makes us feel at home, yet allured by a very different culture. It's that combination that makes the experience of Japanese aesthetics so intoxicating.

How has Japanese design influenced your approach at Norm Architects?

Having now visited and worked in the country for many years, Japanese aesthetics have increasingly made an impact on how we develop and detail many of our projects, from how we work with light and shadow all the way down to the smallest wooden joints.

While we are equally inspired by other design movements and architectural traditions across the world, we always try to work with the spirit of each site, trying to interpret the local ways of building and use local materials to integrate the project seamlessly with its surroundings. However, we are not afraid to use distinct Japanese ideas or elements in a Scandinavian project if it makes sense—and it often does. There is something about the way that traditional Japanese architecture perfectly balances a natural, cool, dry, subtle, and minimalist approach with a super refined, delicate, staged, and orderly aesthetic that makes simple works of architecture very interesting.

What has been your experience of working in Japan—both with Karimoku Case Study with Keiji Ashizawa, and others?

Working in Japan is both difficult and easy at the same time. Aesthetically I feel we understand each other very well and share an appreciation for many of the same qualities of architecture and craft tradition. There might be small differences in perception; for example, Western culture has a tradition of symmetry, but asymmetry is deeply rooted in Japanese aesthetics. Where we sometimes prefer layering of spaces and objects in interiors to create "hygge," the Japanese idea of *ma* (void) is sparser.

How can Japanese and Scandinavian minimalism be used to design for well-being?

It is about accommodating people through empathetic design, rather than treating them as mere spectators of an aesthetic creation—that is key in both traditions. We consider our work as a facilitator of well-being, as a distillation of aesthetics that resonate with the given person and place, and as a system that supports universal human needs. Each project—whether architecture, interiors, or design—is imbued with this intrinsic quality: a simplicity that carries bigger ideas.

Underscoring all of this is perhaps our greatest influence of all: nature. We find ourselves returning again and again to the natural world—the primordial home of the human race—for guidance in the pursuit of timeless beauty, simplicity, and connectivity. Many ancient cultures across the globe have preached the notion that simplicity leads to inner peace and contentment, but in Japanese Zen aesthetics stillness is a central component—the idea that the human mind needs quiet to focus on what is truly meaningful and joyful.

We use sensory materials that remind us of nature and therefore calm us. In our essentialist design approach, decoration is not as taboo as the minimalists insist, but is used with great restraint so as not to dominate the space. It is always authentic to the context and inhabitant, and it's there to add warmth and personality rather than clutter.

In this way, every object serves its user. When taken as a whole, the home becomes the background to an autonomous life.

Simplicity can sometimes be laborious and luxurious. It is more difficult to be selective than it is to be excessive, and it takes a great deal of skill to craft spaces and furniture that work well while hiding everything except the essentials. Every joint, connection, and detail is intentional and finely tuned. If the design reduces itself to its essence and nothing more, and if it is made intentionally, we're often choosing a more sustainable path.

Tactility and natural light seem to be important components of your projects at Norm Architects. How do you imbue spaces with a haptic quality?

The anatomy of a building gives the human body a frame of reference for interaction and meaning. As the body moves through it, the architecture directs our emotions and behaviors through the qualities of its openings, closures, and cavities. We sense our relationship to the scale of a space or height of a room. In the pursuit of well-being through design, then, it is essential to work with space from a perspective that is both poetic and embodied—not just mathematical. As with art, the work needs to be perceived and interpreted by the body if it is going to move us.

Rather than discussing design exclusively in terms of geometry, size, and material, we should adopt a more poetic and philosophical language that addresses the experience, atmosphere, and meaning of spaces. We can measure both the square meters and the emotional weight of a room: it can be small and intimate, or large and impressive. The spatial flow can make sense and please the senses. It is about finding the optimal balance between what we find to be practical on the one hand, and stimulating and comfortable on the other.

Why do you think Japanese design is a particular focus for Scandinavian architects and designers right now?

The focus in Japan on functionality, simplicity, and craft tradition continues to impress and echo the ethos of Danish design. It is this design culture, based in skilled craft tradition and high-quality materials, that continues to attract. Instead of using the word "inspiration" it might be more on point to describe it as an "aesthetic kinship."

EMBRACING IMPERFECTION

Perfection can hold us to such high standards and be so unattainable that it often becomes a barrier to true contentment, both in our lives and in our homes. A Japandi interior takes the idea that there is an ephemeral, almost poetical, appeal to imperfection. Blemishes are seen as beautiful and the organic is valued over uniformity.

The Japanese philosophy of wabi sabi prompts us to remember that all things—including ourselves—go through a process of aging and decay. In this way, it can be said that there are inherent flaws in everything—nothing is ever truly perfect. Wabi sabi is the idea that imperfection is not only unavoidable, it adds extra layers of intrigue, compelling you to touch a material or look a bit closer. As Yanagi Sōetsu, father of the Japanese craft movement, said, "The precise and perfect carries no overtones, admits of no freedom; the perfect is static and regulated, hard and cold. We in our own human imperfections are repelled by the perfect."

Japandi style is the opposite of vulgarity and ostentation. It takes a humbler approach that seeks to not only accept but highlight daily wear and tear, from the hairline fracture in a cup to the well-worn arm of a much-loved chair. It's almost as if the patina of time brings us closer to an object, creating an emotional connection that sparks something deep within. This way of thinking can help us become more content with what is already around us.

Natural Materials

With the apparent simplicity of Japandi interiors, the focus turns naturally to the material palette used in them. Through the layering of textured wood, bamboo, paper, natural textiles, and organic fibers, there is a rich tactility to these spaces that appeals to all the senses. This helps to create earthy, inviting spaces with a worn, rustic beauty.

You will not see any superfluous details or visual trickery in a Japandi space. The choice of the natural over the artificial or synthetic is partly aesthetic, but it's mostly concerned with the desire to express truth and honesty. These are materials that aren't trying to be anything they're not. There's nothing fake about their surface detail or textural quality. They're not shiny, glossy, or shouting for attention. Instead, materials in a Japandi interior are mostly unrefined, rough, and raw, treated with as little intervention as possible. By presenting materials in their true form, it allows us to seek a closer connection to nature and bring an element of the outside in.

Natural materials manage to appeal to something deep within us, when we had a more symbiotic relationship with nature. In today's urban spaces, we're increasingly surrounded by artificiality, sleek technology, and man-made surfaces that have disconnected us from our roots. Often it can lend a feeling of deception, where we're not quite sure if spaces are what they seem. Natural materials, on the other hand, feel safe and familiar. They have a warmth to them. Our nervous system can settle because we recognize their form and texture. Think about running your hand over the timeworn grooves of a wooden table, sinking into softly creased linen sheets, or feeling the smooth, matte texture of stone beneath your bare feet. Spaces that incorporate natural materials simply feel grounding and calming to be in.

HISTORY AND BACKGROUND

Natural materials have been used in Japan and Scandinavia for millennia because, for the most part, that is what has been most readily available. Both regions have abundant areas of forest—making up around seventy percent of the land area in both cases—that they could utilize as a resource to build homes and construct furniture. This helped place a high value on the use of natural materials and a well-rooted respect for their inherent characteristics. With a reliance on materials such as wood and bamboo, local craftspeople could really refine their art and become world experts in one material.

In both regions, this connection with nature fostered a conscious way of thinking about the planet's resources before it even became a cause for concern. Natural materials are, mostly, more sustainable than anything that is man made. You can trace where they come from, they will biodegrade, and they can be easily repaired or recycled. Bamboo, for example, grows quickly without the need for fertilizers or pesticides, and can be cut like grass to enable it to regenerate over and over again. It also absorbs carbon dioxide, uses less water than cotton, and produces more oxygen than a forest of trees.

Historically, Japanese homes have been typically made entirely out of wood. Unlike in the West, stone tended to be used just for foundations or temple podiums. Not only were wooden structures durable enough to withstand unpredictable earthquakes, seasonal storms, and typhoons, they also allowed for the creation of breathable spaces that could suit the changeable humid climate and allow for the flow of air. Traditional Japanese wooden houses tend to be raised slightly off the ground, with an exaggerated, curved roof, oversized eaves, and moveable internal partitions that divide up rooms. They typically have bamboo ceilings, bare neutral walls, paper *shoji* screens, and straw tatami mats on the floor. The muted, minimalist setting, free of adornment and clutter, brings a unique focus to the qualities of the materials.

Instead of using nails or glue, the Japanese traditionally use a system called Tokyō, where wooden blocks and brackets interlock to create strong, sturdy joints and frames. The aim is always to refine the design so it uses fewer materials and embraces what is available. Any wood is typically left unpainted and uncovered, so that the true nature and beauty of the material can be appreciated. The construction of a space also isn't concealed; beams and supports are left exposed as a mark of their function and purpose.

While Japan valued the lightweight qualities of wood, in the West there was more of a reliance on solid stone and brick. This signifies a key difference in thinking between Japan and Scandinavia—with natural disasters built into the way of living with the environment, the Japanese came to see buildings as inherently impermanent and temporary in nature. Wooden homes weren't built to last forever. Nowhere is this more apparent than at Ise Jingū, Japan's oldest shrine, which is torn down and meticulously rebuilt every twenty years at great cost and with elaborate ceremony. The tradition, now in its sixty-second iteration, is seen as a way to preserve craft tradition and pass down wooden building techniques from generation to generation.

The Scandinavians, too, make extensive use of wood in their homes, having long established themselves as world-class cabinet makers renowned for their well-crafted, functional wooden furniture. In the postwar period there was a mutually beneficial relationship between Japan and the Nordic countries, which saw the Japanese government invite Scandinavian designers such as Kaj Franck and Poul Kjærholm over to lecture, while sending students and researchers to Denmark and Finland to learn how things were made there.

For both Japanese and Scandinavian designers, there has long been a desire to push a material to its limits and distill a structure down to its bare essence. Take, for example, Alvar Aalto, who experimented with bent plywood in the 1930s, molding beech wood into shapes that had never been possible. Or Japanese designer Sori Yanagi who, following a Japanese state-sponsored trip to visit Charles and Ray Eames in the US, came back and created the iconic Butterfly Stool in 1954, formed of two curved pieces of plywood held together by metal bolts. While Japanese architecture might have been transient in nature, these designs were built to last and still appear contemporary today.

COMBINING NATURAL MATERIALS

The Japandi style blends natural materials together to create rich layers of texture. Mixing different wood finishes, for example, can help give a space a greater sense of warmth and character. When pairing woods together, try to make sure that there is a contrast between them, for example in tone or texture. It will allow each wood to have its own presence, rather than trying to match them and failing to do so. For example, you might have pale oak flooring with oak kitchen cabinets in a darker stain. What's important is that even if they're different in tone, they have a similar finish—so they might both be matte or glossy. It also helps to consider the undertone of the wood and pair accordingly, depending on whether the undertones are on the warmer or cooler end of the spectrum. For example, a red-toned wood would work with a yellow-toned wood, but if you added in a cooler gray-toned wood, it might make the red one look bright and the gray one chilly.

You can also use rugs to separate different woods, so your eye has something else to rest on. If you're using a lot of wood in your home, try to break it up and distribute it evenly around a space. This repetition will help give a feeling of balance and cohesion. If you have a wooden armchair you might pick up the same wooden tone with a wooden picture frame on the wall above it. A good guide is to stick to a maximum of two to three wood tones in one room.

KEY MATERIALS

Bamboo
With a greater tensile strength than steel, bamboo is known for its durability and versatility. Bamboo can be used to make everything from tableware and everyday utensils, to slatted screens and wall coverings.

Wood
Wood is held in great reverence by both regions. The Japanese typically use Japanese cypress, cherry, and cedar wood, while the Scandinavians rely on oak, birch, beech, and ash. A contemporary Japandi interior might feature wooden shutters, whitewashed wooden floors, and rustic wooden furniture.

Paper
Paper was highly regarded by Japanese designers for its malleability and translucency, which allowed for the creation of opaque screens and rice paper lanterns that could gently diffuse light in a space.

Textiles
Coarse weaves and naturally dyed fabrics are a mainstay of Japandi design, whether that's with woven wall hangings, relaxed linen bedding, or hand-knitted throws.

Tatami
Made of multilayered rice straw topped with natural soft rush, Tatami is a staple in many Japanese homes. Available in three sizes, tatami mats were traditionally used as a unit of measurement to describe the size of a room and typically cover the whole surface area of the floor.

Rattan
Like bamboo, rattan is fast-growing and hard-wearing, using the strands of palms to weave practical forms. It is most typically used for rustic baskets and lampshades.

Jute
Jute is a nontoxic, renewable, and biodegradable plant fiber that can be handwoven to make a tough, thickly textured fabric. Jute rugs are great for those with allergies because they repel dust mites and dirt, rather than holding them in their structure like wool or cotton.

Clay
Arakabe is a traditional Japanese plastering technique that layers rough mud plaster made of clay and straw onto a bamboo lath wall, creating a highly textural and sometimes cracked surface.

Cork
Thanks to its cellular structure, made up of lots of little cells that are filled with air, cork is a great acoustic and thermal insulator, holding warmth longer than other materials such as timber or laminate. It can help dull the sound of steps and absorb loud bangs, creating a calm and peaceful environment.

Concrete
Concrete found popularity in the postwar period when there was a need for inexpensive building materials. Often you will see the imprint of the wooden boards used to cast the concrete, giving the surface a lineated textural quality.

Lime-washed walls

Instead of flat matte paint, consider using a textured limewash paint to bring an aged, chalky finish to your walls, where you can see the marks of the brushstrokes. It will help give a space that lived-in feel. Naturally nontoxic, breathable, and eco-friendly, limewash is traditionally made from crushed limestone mixed with water and natural color pigments. Limewash can be easy to do yourself, but you do need a bit of patience—walls will first need to be prepared with a primer and prep coat before using a large brush to build up light layers of brushstrokes that get roughly blended together.

Wood grain

The whorls and knots of natural wood grain should be celebrated and sought after, and not just in your furniture. Choose wooden cabinet fronts with long bar handles for your kitchen over plain neutral ones, line alcoves with wooden joinery, and even consider a wooden ceiling for maximum coziness.

Linen curtains

A lot of Scandinavian homes typically don't have window treatments, embracing a need to gain as much daylight as possible, but a simple, sheer linen curtain in a neutral color can do a lot to add some material softness to a space. This is especially the case in new-build spaces where there might be a lot of clean, straight, architectural lines. Install a discreet ceiling track for a simple, unobtrusive look.

Rugs

The natural pattern of a rug can help make a space feel more inviting and soften sounds. The softness and thickness of a rug will depend on the pile (the density of the woven fibers that make up its surface). A short pile rug is more practical for high traffic areas, while thick, shaggy rugs can be used in living rooms and bedrooms to add a more luxurious quality.

Wood paneling

Add depth to spaces and create an architectural feature with slatted wood paneling. Slats can be easily purchased as DIY wall panels, with a felt backing that has the additional benefit of acting as a sound insulator. Panels can be installed as part of a media unit or for a bedroom headboard, for example. Separate wooden slats can also be used as room dividers or in place of a traditional stair bannister.

Bathrooms

In bathroom spaces you can add texture with small-format kit kat (finger mosaic) tiles or fluted styles. Use a grout that is slightly darker than your tiles to emphasize the formation of the lines.

Asymmetry and Irregularity

One of the key characteristics of the *wabi sabi* aesthetic is a preference for the asymmetrical. To Japanese Zen masters, irregular compositions were far more appealing to the eye than the order and grandeur of the traditional Western aesthetic. In Japanese design, symmetry was actively avoided in preference for the randomness and unpredictability that can be found in nature.

It was Japanese philosopher Shin'ichi Hisamatsu who said that symmetry was "boring to the mind and deadens the senses." One of seven Japanese aesthetic principles that he defined in 1971, *fukinsei* describes the beauty of asymmetry and irregularity. The idea is that visual harmony and balance can be found when you break away from rigidity and embrace the perfectly imperfect. From a *wabi sabi* sense, this would mean anything that is misshapen, malformed, or jagged. These characteristics somehow capture a feeling of spontaneity, as if things have fallen into place by chance, just as they would in the natural world.

Asymmetry can be found in the texture of natural materials as well as the way you arrange your space. Symmetrical designs can often come across as too contrived, while asymmetrical arrangements might appear more relaxed. The secret is almost making it look as if you haven't tried. It is well known in the interior design world, for example, that arrangements grouped in odd numbers are more aesthetically pleasing. If you're styling shelves or the surface of a sideboard, cluster objects of different heights in groups of three to create balance. You can also hang a piece of art slightly off center above a sofa or dining table, or pair mismatching armchairs with a sofa to make it feel less formal. Somehow asymmetry makes a space feel more livable, rather than a stage set that you can't touch.

Pattern

Compared to more maximalist spaces where ornament is king, pattern isn't an obvious element of Japandi interiors. That's not to say it isn't there, you just need to know where to look. In Japanese and Scandinavian design, you will find a quieter nod to pattern that is more subtly expressed in the weave of textiles, the folds of fabric, and the uneven texture of materials as well as occasionally in more obvious places, such as with graphic art prints and decorative wallpaper. The emphasis will nearly always be on simplicity and purity of expression.

In Japandi design, pattern, if there's any at all, takes inspiration directly from nature. Traditional Japanese art would typically feature decorative motifs depicting flowing water, waves, unfurling petals, and flying birds. More often than not these motifs would be imbued with a feeling of movement, creating a sense of life and vitality. Japanese philosopher Yanagi Sōetsu said that pattern teaches us how to perceive nature: "Through patterns we are able to see nature for the first time," he said. "Nature then appears more mysterious than ever before. An era without good patterns is an era that is not looking attentively at nature." To him, pattern was the portrayal of the essence of something, reduced to its primary elements. In its most simple form, it might be the intricate knots of a woven rug or the natural dye of a piece of fabric.

The Scandinavians too, are well versed in representing nature in pattern. Take Finnish brand Marimekko as an example. Founded in Helsinki in 1951 by Viljo and Armi Ratia, Marimekko expressed the free-spirited, progressive nature of the postwar period with abstract shapes and bold, reduced forms that are still popular today. Their enduring classics include a plain stripe design by Vuokko

Nurmesniemi and the graphic Unikko poppy by Maija Isola. Also in Finland, architect Alvar Aalto created the geometric Siena textile pattern, a monochrome design formed of repetitive black bars. In Sweden in the 1930s, Josef Frank fused fantasy and nature into botanical patterns for Svenskt Tenn, while in Denmark in the 1940s, Arne Jacobsen based his plant motifs for textiles and wallpaper designs on nature studies he carried out in the Swedish landscape.

TRADITIONAL JAPANESE PATTERNS

Seigaiha
A repetitive fan-shaped design that references the waves of the sea; water being a symbol of good luck in Japan.

Yagasuri
Depicts the shapes of bird feathers that were used on the tips of arrows. It was traditionally reproduced as a symbol of protection for the kimonos of new brides.

Asanoha
A star-shaped pattern that represents hemp leaves. Hemp was more commonly used in Japan until cotton was imported.

Igeta
A delicate pattern that draws similarities with the hash symbol, said to represent a well that symbolizes life.

Kanoko
This dotted pattern, resembling the spots on a fawn's back, is made by tightly knotting fabric and using a complex shibori dyeing technique.

Ichimatsu
A simple checkered design usually composed of two contrasting colors.

Shippo
A circular pattern that represents the seven treasures of Buddhism and is regarded as a symbol of harmony.

Same komon
Formed of small dots arranged in overlapping arcs, referencing a shark's skin.

Tsuru
This pattern features the crane, a graceful bird that symbolizes good fortune and longevity in Japanese culture.

Sakura
Japan's national emblem, the cherry blossom, marks the change in seasons and acts as a reminder of the fleeting, ever-changing beauty of nature.

Broken but Beautiful

Kintsugi is the Japanese art of repairing broken pottery or ceramics with lacquer dusted in powdered gold or silver. Instead of throwing something away if it gets damaged or breaks, you are encouraged to put it back together, and in the process, actively celebrate the object's imperfections. Any defects are seen as a blessing in disguise—something to be valued and celebrated, rather than concealed or forgotten. The mended object takes on even greater meaning because you've added to the story of its life. As with *wabi sabi*, we can use *kintsugi* as a metaphor for life, understanding that our flaws only make us stronger.

The practice of *kintsugi* can be used to fix cracks and chips in ceramic and porcelain plates, cups, jugs, and other broken objects. It's about giving something meaning and purpose again. In a similar way to *ikebana*, the Japanese art of flower arranging (see pages 128–30), there is a sense of mindfulness in the practice. Through the action of mending, there is an emotional process that forces you to pause, slow down, and practice carefulness as you piece together the fragments and reconnect with the once-damaged object. A full *kintsugi* repair is a slow process, taking from a couple of months to a year to execute properly. As with all Japanese arts, it is not to be hurried.

The art of *kintsugi* is thought to have come out of the Japanese tea ceremony, which was defined by a very particular *wabi sabi* way of thinking. From the 15th century, the tea masters of Japan rejected perfection and sought out cups and pots that embodied imperfection with irregular shapes, variable glazes, and hairline fissures that resulted from the firing process. They didn't just make do with these little mistakes, they took them as a truer expression of beauty, one

that brought them closer to nature. For them, beauty hid behind irregularity and it took the viewer to draw it out of the object. Slowly over time, this idea filtered down into more mundane, everyday objects that you might use at home. As such, it relates to the Japanese word *shibui*, which describes a simple, unobtrusive beauty that can be found in everything from a person to an interior space. Something is considered *shibui* if it is humble, authentic, and without any need for superfluous decoration. While Kintsugi is a traditional Japanese practice, it is now becoming more accessible to all thanks to online courses, workshops, and DIY kits that you can use to mend objects at home in your own time.

THE PROCESS OF *KINTSUGI*

Observation

Evaluate the cracks and fractures that need repair and make a map of the piece. The Japanese believe that the mending process is a deeply personal experience, and your personality or emotions are often reflected in the design. The method you use will also depend on whether you're reattaching broken shards, filling in an empty chip, or touching up smaller fissures.

Pretreatment and preparation

A filing tool is used to prepare and smooth the rough surface of any broken edges or fissure lines. Sandpaper can also be used for more delicate work.

Gluing back together

Traditional *kintsugi* uses *urushi* lacquer, which comes from the toxic sap of the urushi tree. It is usually mixed with rice glue, flour, or clay powder to create a durable adhesive. *Urushi* can be difficult to use, not to mention hard to get hold of outside Japan, so some people choose to use epoxy resin instead.

Assembly

Hold the pieces in place until the lacquer or resin hardens. Once hardened, you should scrape off any excess glue that has oozed out of the cracks to ensure a smooth finish. Traditional *urushi* lacquer needs humidity to dry and pots are usually left for a few days in a *urushi-buro*, a wooden box used for curing.

Lacquering

In traditional *kintsugi*, the colors red and black are used to symbolize the natural cycle of life and death. Black *urushi* is first delicately painted onto the fractures to pay respect to the broken piece. The application of red *urushi* is then said to give it a new lease of life. After each step the lacquer is shaved down and polished.

Finishing touches

A gold or silver powder called *kinpun* is carefully applied onto wet lacquer. Instead of rough cracks, you will now see beautiful glistening seams running across your vessel.

Time Itself is an Art

AN INTERVIEW WITH IRENE CHANG, FOUNDER OF MAANA HOMES

Seeking to create experiences inspired by the art of slow living, luxury hospitality brand Maana Homes was founded by creatives Irene Chang and Hana Tsukamoto in 2017. With a collection of ancient *machiya* guesthouses (traditional wooden homes) spread across Kyoto, painstakingly restored with the help of architect Shigenori Uoya, they aim to bring a warm feeling of home to everything they do. Connecting past and present, their approach carefully balances a respect for heritage with a gentle nod to modern living. While each of their homes tells a different story, inspired by the context of their unique setting, they are all designed for moments of quiet contemplation. For them, the beauty of Japanese design comes from looking within, where everyday life becomes a form of meditation.

Can you tell me the story behind Maana Homes?

Hana and I both went to school in California, US, and were childhood friends. She went on to become a creative director in New York, and I stayed in LA to do hotel interior architecture, but we would often travel together. We wanted to create a meaningful hospitality brand that would change the conversation around luxury travel. All these higher-end hotels are essentially the same kind of thing, but I feel like people crave experiences and connections that have some sort of depth; that inspire a new understanding or perspective of a place. That's a new luxury.

Maana Homes creates spaces that "inspire the mind and calm the heart." Could you explain your design approach?

It's really about balancing inspiration and warmth. Hana and I talked about some of the memories that really touched our hearts or moved us, and it was always places that felt very warm. Our design approach is about creating a sense of calm and a feeling like you're coming home. It's not so much a stylistic thing—the whole brand of Maana to me is really about exploring what it means to live well. One of the ways we can do that is just by being aware of simple everyday moments. It's so apparent when you live in Kyoto because that is the way of life here. Everything is so intentional, whether you're making a coffee, or lighting incense, or sitting down to chat with a loved one. It's a moment of self-care and it's so luxurious now to have this time to yourself. Our design approach is about creating these special moments at home.

What does wabi sabi mean to you?

It's a philosophy; in its simplest term you can call it embracing imperfection. To me, it's really a lifelong practice. As a designer, you have to let go of the idea of perfection. Everything in the future is going to be automated and everyone's always striving for the perfect, but what makes us human is our flaws and imperfection. To really truly understand that you have to take a step back, and just allow something to be the way it is and constantly remind yourself that's what makes it beautiful. For example, our floors are really beaten up right now; do we fix them or leave the patina as it is? It's these really small decisions that make up the philosophy.

At Maana, we love time-worn textures and tactility. There's so many materials in a Japanese house that just aren't used in modern houses anymore, such as the earthen clay wall. The craft has sort of been lost in modern architecture. But there are studies that show that these sorts of textures and the shadows on the walls actually calm our mental state, especially if it is a natural material. The science and the heritage is there, but it's become a little disconnected from the modern world.

Japanese interiors seem to balance function and poetic beauty so well. What do you think is the secret?

I would say it's the Japanese focus on the inner world more than the outer world. In the West, it's all about embellishment and adding layers of interesting things. But in Japanese homes, the lack of embellishment is so intentional and there's such a connection to nature, and also to yourself. Japanese *machiya* are a lesson in restraint. A single piece of art or flower, is intentionally positioned (typically in a *tokonoma*, or recess) to command the room's full attention, inviting deep contemplation of the piece. Everything is there for a reason; from the windows and how they frame views, to every material and texture used.

What inspiration have you taken from Scandinavian design and interiors?

I think Scandinavian design also has the same intention, with that idea of seamlessness and hiding all the hardware of a building. But it's really interesting because visually they're so extreme—Japanese design is so moody and textural, while Scandinavian design is so light and clean. Japanese interiors tend to be darker and more muted, with more square shapes and less color. We're experimenting by adding more curves and I feel like the contrast is really interesting together. The underlying core is still the same; there's a commitment to craft tradition, quality, and detail.

What do you think Japanese design can teach us about embracing imperfection?

I think it's important to understand that flaws and imperfections can be seen as beautiful. When you stay in these one-hundred-year-old homes of ours, sometimes it's not a perfect experience; sometimes it's a little bit cold or the walls are a bit crumbly, but ultimately you look at it and see that's what gives the space its overall uniqueness.

The same can be said about the art of kintsugi, that it can teach us to accept our own flaws, do you agree?

I think there's something beautifully impermanent about the passage of time. Only time can really give you that sort of weathered beauty. You can't really re-create that. When you practice *kintsugi* it's something like an eight-week process. You can love a bowl that you buy and spend a lot of money on, but when you spend eight weeks repairing that bowl, it takes on a whole new meaning, because you invested time into it. The cracks represent the time and love you've invested into the piece and that is irreplaceable. That comes back to ourselves in some ways. Western society has such a complex about aging, but it should really be the opposite. As time goes on, you pick up all of these wrinkles and scars and imperfections, or the gold cracks in a piece of ceramic, and it's beautiful, and should be celebrated. Every passing of time is so unique on its own. It's like time itself is an art.

A CONNECTION TO NATURE

Japan and Scandinavia share an abundance of nature on their doorstep, which has shaped both their design histories and national identities. Each culture shares a strong sense of maintaining equilibrium and harmony with nature so that everyone can continue to enjoy the benefits for generations to come.

Scandinavian designers have long been inspired by the purity of natural forms, while Japanese houses were traditionally designed in relation to the outside environment. But this respect for nature runs deeper than the spaces they inhabit. In Japanese folklore kodama are the spirits said to inhabit trees, and today numerous trees are considered sacred and protected. In Sweden, more trees are grown than are cut down, and it is now covered by more forest today than it was a century ago.

The belief in the restorative power of nature filters into daily life too. Scandinavians will be out in all weathers, they'll gather with friends at summer houses and go wild swimming in their city waterways and archipelago lakes. In Japan, nature is everywhere, from tiny urban gardens that spill from doorsteps onto the street to the ikebana floral arrangements that decorate small spaces. The thinking is that nature can help reset the mind and renew our mood. Now that we spend most of our time indoors, it is more important than ever that we find ways to reconnect with nature and create spaces that make us feel grounded.

Biophilic Design

Biophilia is the idea that, as humans, we have an innate, evolutionary predisposition to recognize and relate to the natural world. We tend to be drawn to natural motifs or materials and feel instantly calmer when surrounded by nature. It goes back to something primal within us, when we were more at one with the natural world. Biophilic design principles, which can be found in Japandi interiors, have been shown to reduce stress, boost mood, and increase feelings of relaxation. Studies have shown, for example, that sleeping in a wooden bed can help reduce your heart rate.

Biophilia quite literally translates "as a love of nature." The word derives from *bio* meaning "life and living things," and the Greek *philia* meaning "fondness." When it comes to interior design, it means taking inspiration from nature to create healthy, soothing spaces that are designed for comfort and well-being. It is more than just adding plants, although that can certainly help to bring vibrancy and life to neutral surroundings. As we have seen with design for the senses (see page 46), biophilia is very much focused on the experience of a space. Biophilic design suggests that there is an emotional connection between nature and humans—it's also about feeling at home in a place and it's true that often nature has the power to bring us back to ourselves. We know we feel good when we're outside, even if it's just a quick walk around the park during our lunch hour, so it makes sense that we might want to capture that restorative feeling and create a refuge from the stress of urban modern living. And it's not just all in our head—scientific research has shown that hospital patients recover more quickly with a green view and that wooden interiors can help to reduce blood pressure.

Japanese and Scandinavian designers have long been using biophilic design principles, without really giving it a name. Nature has always been the inspiration and sustainability has continued to be an integral factor in the design process. As well as taking direct inspiration from nature, with the aforementioned use of plants, for example, biophilic design principles use indirect references and elements that mimic the things you might see in the natural world. Scandinavian interiors, for instance, use light, muted colors, curved forms in their furniture, and natural materials. Japanese design tends to feature raw, primitive textures, an abundance of wood, and moments that symbolically act as a portrayal of nature, such as a piece of art or a stem in a vase.

BIOPHILIC DESIGN PRINCIPLES TO BRING INTO THE HOME

Natural materials

Spaces designed with natural materials, such as wood, have been proven to lower blood pressure and calm the nervous system. This is because they feel grounding and warmer to the touch. Choose solid wood surfaces over faux finishes, natural flooring over artificial tiles, and organic fabrics over synthetic fibers (see pages 66–69).

Texture

Natural materials are rarely uniform and perfect. Prevent a neutral space from seeming dull by embracing the texture and tactility you would find in the natural world. In Japandi spaces this can be done with jute rugs, thickly woven throws, and wrinkled linen.

Natural motifs

Take inspiration from the intricate shapes and forms that can be found in nature. Fractals are infinitely complex patterns that form the structure of leaves, tree branches, and even our own lungs. Scientists believe that because we evolved in a fractal world surrounded by nature, we are better able to recognize natural forms and scenes, and find them relaxing. It's easy to introduce subtle references to natural motifs in your artwork and accessories.

Biomorphic forms

These are shapes that are abstract yet reminiscent of the contours or textures you might find in natural forms and living organisms, such as those in rock formations, seashells, sand dunes, and animal skins. These elements tend to be defined by the golden ratio, a concept that is found throughout nature and is thought to be visually pleasing to the human eye. You can introduce fluid, natural forms into your space with sculptural pendant lights, abstract wallpaper, and patterned rugs.

Curves

Break up the straight lines and harsh architectural features of a home with organic curves inspired by nature. Studies have shown that curved rooms are perceived as more inviting and calming than those with angular forms (see page 121).

Indoor plants

Bring nature into the home in the most literal way with houseplants and fresh greenery. Plants not only help to purify the air, they have also been shown to reduce stress levels and improve productivity in work spaces.

Natural light

Just like plants, we too need natural light. The bright, airy spaces of Scandinavian interiors make us feel good because they're uplifting and energizing. Carefully consider window treatments and arrange your furniture to optimize the best pockets of light.

Views of nature

Studies have connected the use of green views with reduced anger and improved happiness. The calming effects of viewing nature work just as well when applied to images of nature as with actual views of real nature, showing that even small urban spaces can benefit from plants, natural paintings, and green walls.

Natural Light

Scandinavian and Japanese interiors have always been sensitive to natural light. While the Nordic countries tend to try to enhance the amount of light they receive into their homes and create brighter spaces, the Japanese seem to focus on the delicate play of light that filters into the darker recesses of their homes. Both regions understand the mood and feeling that can be created with the right lighting.

We need natural daylight to guide our circadian rhythm, the natural twenty-four-hour cycle that helps us wake up in the morning and feel ready for bed in the evenings. Studies have found that natural light increases serotonin, the happiness hormone that helps regulate our mood and reduce depression. But if we're spending more time indoors than ever before, we're probably not always seeing those benefits. Indeed, we're now becoming more aware of the harmful effects of artificial lighting. We know that if we look at the blue light of our phone late at night, it's probably not going to help our sleep. We might turn off the main ceiling light in the evening because it feels too stark and not very conducive to relaxing. And we also know that sunshine is good for the soul and darker spaces tend to feel a bit more downbeat.

Biophilic design uses inspiration from nature to re-create the pattern and movement of natural light. It's about making sure your home can adapt with you throughout the day. In order to feel at your best, for example, you want to pull back the blinds and curtains and get as much daylight as possible first thing in the morning, even if it's sitting next to a window drinking your morning cup of coffee. As the day progresses and the sun starts to set, consider gradually turning down the lighting and shift lights from alert, bright blue to a warmer orange tone to create a more restful feeling that sets you up for sleep.

You can maximize natural light in your home by adding rooflights and internal glazed partitions, and transom windows above doors. If you're renting or unable to make more invasive changes, use mirrors to bounce light around and choose pale colors to give a feeling of airiness. Also consider ways of introducing moments of light and shadow that have different intensities, to mimic the natural variations of sunlight. Take inspiration from Japanese interiors and use slatted screens and paper lanterns to diffuse light in a gentler form. There's also something instantly calming about the movement of sheer curtains in the breeze.

KOMOREBI

The Japanese concept of *komorebi* translates as "sunlight leaking through the trees." It describes the dancing light and play of shadows that filters through leaves and branches. The beauty of *komorebi* is most evident when you see sunshine casting rays through a forest and is the magical moment when the light seems to hit just right and come alive, and you feel in awe of nature for a second. At its simplest, *komorebi* can be captured inside the home with delicate shadows from plants and flowers. But you can also use decorative privacy film with natural motifs on bathroom windows, install solid or slatted window shutters, or use perforated pendant lights to cast beautiful shadows on the walls.

GETTING THE LIGHTING RIGHT

Layer your lighting

Think of your lighting in terms of layers of intensity and make sure to have a mix of ambient lighting, task lighting, and accent lighting. You need a minimum of four light sources in a room, ideally six or seven for larger rooms. Ambient lighting is your main source of lighting and will give a far-reaching spread of illumination, for example, with a ceiling pendant or chandelier. Task lighting offers brighter, more focused light for activities where you need to be alert, such as the lights around a bathroom mirror or over a kitchen island. Accent lighting is what will create a cozy, inviting feeling in a space, with the use of wall lights, uplighters, and floor or table lamps.

Think about function

Consider what you will be doing in the space and design your lighting according to the ambience you want to create. Reserve bright downlights and spotlights for kitchens and bathrooms, and use softer shades and pendants elsewhere.

Create focal points

Use lamps to create cozy corners in a room, for instance, on a side table next to a sofa or on a sideboard in a dining room.

Install dimmers

A dimmer switch will give you flexibility over your lighting so that you can turn the brightness up or down depending on the time of day.

Smart lighting

Smart light bulbs can be installed in your existing light fittings and be controlled by a remote control or an app on your phone. It allows you to adjust the light and atmosphere in a room to suit your mood, without even needing to get up from the sofa. If you don't want to wire-in light fittings, you can also get battery operated or rechargeable LED bulbs that mimic the look of a traditional filament bulb.

Candlelight

The Scandinavians understand the power of candlelight better than any other region. Lighting a candle is an important part of everyday life and it is even said that they burn more wax than anywhere else in the world! Nothing says cozy, or hygge (the Danish equivalent), like a softly burning candle on a chilly night.

The Joy of Indoor Plants

Indoor plants are a great way to bring the outside in, especially in a Japandi interior that's all bare walls and neutral finishes. You don't need the world's largest space to create an impact with greenery either, there's plenty of easy, affordable ways to create your own urban jungle, whether it's with window boxes, potted herbs, terrariums, or decorative Japanese *kokedamas*.

Houseplants not only help to brighten up the look of your home, they can also uplift your mood and well-being too. Studies have shown that just being around indoor plants can help reduce anxiety and stress, and lower blood pressure. One research study from Japan suggested that leafy plants could even help with creativity when doing simple workplace tasks. It might just be the sight of lush greenery that instantly calms us, or it could be the ritual of taking care of something that forces us to slow down and destress.

Plants have also been shown to help improve indoor air quality—they do this by capturing pollutants, absorbing moisture and mold, and increasing oxygen levels through the natural process of photosynthesis. There was a landmark study by NASA in 1989 that suggested plants could even remove VOCs (volatile organic compounds), including chemicals such as benzene and formaldehyde, which can be found in typical household furnishings made of upholstery foam and MDF. The best air-purifying plants tend to be peace lilies, *Aloe vera*, Boston ferns, spider plants, bamboos, and orchids. One study found that a spider plant can remove up to ninety percent of toxins in the air in just two days.

Start small and know that even a single plant can help elevate an interior. If you're not feeling particularly green-fingered, try some herb boxes on a windowsill or a hardy *Monstera* plant in the corner of your living room. If in doubt, it helps to understand the light conditions that each plant needs. Some plants will thrive in direct light, others will need indirect light to prevent their leaves getting scorched, and some will prefer a shadier spot.

KOKEDAMA

One unique way of bringing the outside in is *kokedama*, which originated in Japan as an offshoot of the art of bonsai. It is a way of displaying indoor plants by wrapping the roots and soil in moss. The word translates as "moss ball." *Kokedama* is best suited to petite plants with small root systems, such as succulents, ferns, ivy, and *Philodendrons*. To make a *kokedama*, mix multi-purpose peat-free compost with bonsai soil or sand and a bit of water until you can form it into a compact ball. Carefully take your chosen plant out of its plastic pot and shake off some of the excess soil. Break your ball of soil in half and firmly mold the two halves around the roots of your plant. You can then cover your ball of soil in preserved sheet moss and hold it in place by wrapping it with gardener's twine. Your *kokedama* can be displayed on a windowsill or hanging from a hook away from direct light. Use a mister to keep your moss ball constantly damp and soak it in a bowl of water for five to ten minutes every now and then. Watch your *kokedama* flourish and enjoy the instantly mood-boosting benefits of nature.

PLANTS FOR A JAPANDI INTERIOR

Swiss cheese plant (*Monstera deliciosa*)
This plant is so-named because of the distinctive holes that mark its broad, heart-shaped leaves. These sprawling tropical plants grow easily and quickly in indirect light, and are perfect for filling corners with a bold punch of lush greenery.

Rubber fig (*Ficus elastica*)
Hailing from Southeast Asia, this tall growing plant has thick, shiny leaves. It's relatively hardy and suitable for most rooms.

Fiddle-leaf fig (*Ficus lyrata*)
A tropical plant with large waxy leaves that thrives in bright, sunny corners away from drafts. Once you find the right spot for it, a *ficus* won't like to be moved.

Asparagus fern (*Asparagus setaceus*)
A delicate-looking fern with feathery sprays of foliage. These ferns can be quite high maintenance and require high humidity, which makes them perfect for a bright bathroom.

**Chinese money plant
(*Pilea peperomioides*)**
A small plant with coin-shaped leaves, native to southern China. It's easy to propagate with cuttings, perhaps explaining its more common nickname.

ZZ plant (*Zamioculcas zamiifolia*)
According to feng shui, the ZZ plant is said to bring good luck and fortune to its owners.

Money tree (*Pachira aquatica*)
Another plant that's popular with proponents of feng shui, it's formed of several trunks that are braided together to symbolize good fortune.

Olive tree (*Olea europaea*)
A small tree traditionally found in the Mediterranean, the olive tree can be grown inside in sunny, south-facing rooms. It's best to move your olive tree outside in the summer months though.

Kentia palm (*Howea forsteriana*)
A very hardy, tolerant palm that is content in shade and can help to improve indoor air quality.

**Japanese bird's nest fern
(*Asplenium antiquum*)**
A fern with curly fronds that will thrive in high-humidity kitchens and bathrooms.

Bonsai tree
Bonsai has come to mean a type of stylized potted plant, but the term actually better describes the Japanese art of growing and shaping miniature trees into beautiful art forms. It translates simply as "planted in a container." Bonsai is an expression of Japanese *wabi sabi* and typically symbolizes harmony, peace, strength, and balance. Grown in shallow containers, bonsai trees need to be watered and fertilized regularly. Looking after a bonsai is seen as a lifelong hobby that requires care and focus.

Restorative Nature

In our fast-paced world, connecting with nature helps us to reset, get offline, and switch off from all the hustle and bustle. From Norway's philosophy of *friluftsliv* to Japan's medicinal practice of forest bathing, the Scandinavians and Japanese have certain rituals built into their cultures that encourage the benefits of simple moments spent outdoors.

By 2050, it is predicted that nearly seventy percent of the world's population will be living in urban areas. The dense, crowded spaces of cities, with excess pollution and noise all make for a stressful experience, where we have become more and more disconnected from what feels natural and grounding. It's not hard to see why we get overwhelmed and burnt out. There might be a simple solution: spending more time in nature. Just looking at nature can reduce our heart rate and decrease anger or aggression. One study in Japan found that viewing a forest landscape for twenty minutes has the power to return us to a relaxed state following a moment of stress, suggesting that we need short, frequent moments in greenery to restore ourselves back to peace.

Japan and Scandinavia can be said to be the original proponents of ecotherapy, the practice of immersing oneself in nature to improve mental and physical health. Ecotherapy can be as simple as walking in nature, meditating outside, or spending time gardening or crafting from natural objects.

FRILUFTSLIV

In Norway, there is the concept of *friluftsliv*, a term conceived by Norwegian playwright Henrik Ibsen in the 1850s to describe the sense of spiritual well-being that can be found from humble moments enjoyed in remote settings. *Friluftsliv* means open-air living and is really about disconnecting from daily stresses, whether that's with a hike in the forest or a digital detox at the weekend. It's understood more widely in Scandinavia as the sharing of a collective culture that sees humans as part of nature. It's an idea that is even ingrained in law— all the Nordic countries allow the right to roam, which is called *friluftsloven* in Norway. It means that everyone can enjoy almost unlimited access to nature, and camp or walk wherever they please, as long as they do so responsibly. In Norway, there's even a dedicated association called *Norsk Friluftsliv* with more than 5,000 outdoor clubs to encourage the idea of outdoor living.

Not everyone has access to an outside space or garden though, so it's about appreciating those moments where we can. Even our homes can become a natural respite from it all if we bring nature inside.

FOREST BATHING

Forest bathing, or *shinrin yoku*, is a mindfulness practice that originated in Japan in the 1980s as a remedy for depression. It is spending time in a forest and really taking in what's around you, allowing you to get into a meditative space where your senses take over. Instead of just marching through a forest from point A to B, forest bathing requires a bit of focus and reflection. It's the act of slowing down and mindfully observing your surroundings, down to the smallest detail. Turn off your phone or leave it at home, take a few deep breaths, run your hand over the bark of a tree, listen to the rustle of the wind in the leaves, or even sit down for a moment. Embrace the rhythms of nature and allow all your stress to wash away.

The advantages of forest bathing are so respected in Japan that it's even prescribed as preventative healthcare. It has been shown to improve sleep, reduce stress hormone production, boost the immune system, and aid happiness.

We can carry the idea of forest bathing with us throughout the day and into our homes. That could mean making a ritual out of watering your plants each week, sitting in a window seat and appreciating the change in seasons, or foraging for branches and elements of nature to decorate your home with. The bathroom is the perfect place to recreate the healing feeling of forest bathing. Ferns, *Philodendrons*, ivies, and snake plants will all thrive in the humid environment of a bathroom. A bunch of fresh *Eucalyptus* hung up in the shower can also release a soothing fragrance and will last for months. Or simply take take a moment out of your week to re-create a spa-like experience—light a

candle, even if it's just for a shower, switch off all technology, and create your own sensory experience. You don't have to step into a forest to feel the benefits.

SHIZEN

Along with *kanso* (simplicity) and *fukinsei* (irregularity), *shizen* is one of seven Japanese aesthetic principles that defines the *wabi sabi* style. The dictionary defines it as "nature" or "naturalness." But unlike the Western idea of nature, *shizen* also describes things that are man-made but designed to look like they've come from nature, such as golf courses and Japanese Zen gardens. As such, it's also about how we interpret nature and blend our homes with our surroundings. An interior can be considered *shizen* if it captures the effortlessness of nature, for example, with local materials, unpretentious details, and natural textures.

Natural Roots

AN INTERVIEW WITH MARIANNE GOEBL, DIRECTOR OF ARTEK

Alvar Aalto was a pioneering Finnish architect and designer known for his human-centric approach to design, typically using organic forms and natural materials to create warm, light-filled spaces inspired by nature. Aalto conceived each of his buildings as a complete work of art, designing furniture as well as light fixtures and glassware, often in collaboration with his first wife, Aino Aalto. Together with Aino, Maire Gullichsen, and Nils-Gustav Hahl, he founded furniture company Artek in 1935. Today the brand continues Aalto's story, building on values of clarity, functionality, and poetic simplicity. Here Marianne Goebl, managing director of Artek, describes how Artek is intrinsically and historically connected to nature.

Looking back at the history of Artek, do you know how much inspiration Alvar Aalto took from Japan? Did he ever visit the country?

While Alvar and Aino Aalto never visited Japan in person, they were well aware of Japanese architecture and design. Their office library contained books on Japanese building techniques and craftsmanship, and they referenced Japanese influences a lot. Looking at their furniture designs, the Tea Trolley, one of Aalto's most cherished designs, is said to be inspired by British tea culture and Japanese woodwork.

In the early 1930s, the Aaltos developed a personal friendship with the Japanese ambassador to Finland and his wife, Mr. and Ms. Ichikawa. Ms. Ichikawa gave Aino Aalto a silk fabric with a cherry blossom—*kirsikankukka* in Finnish—motif. Delighted and inspired, Aino created her own *kirsikankukka* pattern as an homage to Japanese textile design. The pattern was printed on cotton fabric and used for curtains, tablecloths, and cushions.

Artek has described the friendship between Finland and Japan as a "unique soulmate relationship." What do you think connects Japan and Finland so well?

Despite their geographical separation, Finland and Japan share a deep kinship; both enjoy the essence of a simple life and long for the integration of nature in all aspects of the quotidian. They share a love of silence, a reduced visual language, and a deep respect for craftsmanship, resulting in a genuine appreciation for a certain "quality of imperfection," which does not only allow for, but cherishes irregularities in products made from natural materials.

With the FIN/JPN Friendship Collection, introduced in 2019 to celebrate one hundred years of diplomatic relations between Finland and Japan, Artek aimed to epitomize these qualities. Traditional Japanese craft techniques, such as indigo dye or a combination of wood sanding techniques, were applied to classic Aalto furniture designs in novel ways.

In 2023, we collaborated with Japanese architect Tsuyoshi Tane to celebrate the ninetieth anniversary of Aalto's three-legged Stool 60. The architect explored the aging process of wood and how to gracefully enhance it by burying untreated birch wood in Japanese soils of various colors.

I believe that part of the similarities between Finnish and Japanese culture are anchored in a certain outsider status of both countries. Finland and Japan are situated at the geographic periphery of their respective continent, fully or largely surrounded by water. Both nations are exposed to extreme weather conditions and hence came to embrace nature in a particularly intense way. These aspects, as well as the originality of both countries' languages, led to a certain degree of isolation, which allowed for the development of independent and yet surprisingly compatible lifestyles.

Alvar Aalto was very inspired by natural forms and natural materials—could you say more about how nature informed his work?

Nature's infinite wealth of forms as well as its construction principles clearly influenced his work. It can be seen in Alvar Aalto's use of organic lines, asymmetrical spaces, fan shapes, or undulating ceilings; his "flexible standardization" approach to make components for his furniture; or of course, his choice of materials—stone, brick, and, above all, wood.

Alvar Aalto also had a special understanding of how to harness the power of natural light. How important was that in his work and interiors?

Creating a balanced play between natural and artificial light is central to most architecture in the Nordic countries, where life is marked by long, cold winters with limited daylight and short summers with endless hours of sun. Alvar Aalto, indeed, developed a particularly sophisticated understanding of light. He integrated light into spaces in many different ways, through skylights, hidden windows, or windows reaching over the ceiling level to get the maximum amount of daylight in his spaces.

He also fitted his architectural buildings and private homes with specially designed light fixtures. Considered lighting was an expression of Aalto's human-centric philosophy, and in particular, the idea that well-designed artificial light can bring people closer together and even take on a therapeutic role—particularly in Finland, with its dark winters. In addition to the psychological and optical aspects of light fixtures, Aalto also focused on their sculptural and sensual qualities. A light should look beautiful whether it is on or off, and Aalto's luminaires radiate a gentle light, both direct and indirect, while never exposing the eye directly to the artificial light source. Like the sunlight that falls through the leaves of a tree, the light of his luminaires is soft and diffused.

How does nature continue to influence Artek's designs today?

Artek is intrinsically connected to nature, more specifically to the Finnish forest. More than eighty percent of Artek furniture is made from birch trees grown, felled, and seasoned in Central Finland. The unique solid wood bending techniques, which Aalto had developed using Finnish birch wood and its particular properties, are still at the core of Artek's collection and manufacturing today.

In collaboration with research-based design studio Formafantasma, we have introduced "wild birch," a new wood selection, which allows for knots, insect trails, or darker core wood. Artek currently favors regularly grained wood, a criterion that came from a market expectation for visual consistency in natural materials, but this isn't exactly in line with wood's inherent variability. Applying this new wood selection makes each product different and unique.

Why is this important?

By introducing wild birch, Artek is ensuring that more of the tree is used to produce long-lasting products, in turn maximizing opportunities to store CO_2. The longer a tree is left growing in the forest, the more CO_2 it will store. The birch trees used in Artek furniture are between fifty and eighty years old and absorb CO_2 throughout their lifetime. By embracing more natural features in wood to make long-lasting Artek products, it means that ultimately fewer trees will be cut to make these products.

With the introduction of "wild birch" we aim to shift our customers' attention to how a tree actually looks—full of irregularities—making each tree different, which we consider beautiful. A systemic shift for the entire design industry is necessary toward encompassing greater use of wood as a valuable raw material. Ultimately, wood must be treated like a natural material that's full of individual features rather than a homogenous, regular material.

HARMONY
AND BALANCE

Japandi interiors have an inherent sense of tranquility and serenity to them. Everything is perfectly balanced so as to create a graceful arrangement that settles the eye and calms the soul.

The idea of seeking a peaceful balance is woven into the very core of Japanese culture and aesthetics. The Japanese have a concept called wa, which can be translated simply into the English word "harmony." The concept of wa guides everything from the design of Zen gardens and architectural interiors, to the elegant, poised gestures of the tea ceremony and even the nonconfrontational nature of daily conversations. Scandinavians, too, seek to live in harmony with their surroundings, perfectly encapsulated in the Swedish philosophy of lagom (see page 31).

With interior design, we can use the idea of harmony and balance to create a feeling of unity in our homes. Think of it as if you're creating a conversation between elements. Pare back your color palette and use just one or two accent tones dotted around the room in your accessories and artwork. Or take one shape and repeat the form in different guises throughout the space. This will help tie various elements of a room together and give your eye a recognizable feature to rest on as it travels around the space.

A Neutral Color Palette

Japandi interiors are defined by a considered palette of warm neutrals. This helps to create a versatile, muted backdrop for everyday life to bring the color, texture, and interest. The Japanese and Scandinavians tend to see neutral colors as a more timeless choice, helping to create pared-back elegant spaces that will defy trends and evolve with changing needs or mood. Choosing the right neutral will ultimately help you create a tranquil setting that will feel restful and restorative.

For a Japandi interior, beige is never boring. Instead there is a nuance of tone and texture that brings tactility to a space. Often the inspiration comes from the natural world, whether that's the sandy tones of beach dunes, the oatmeal hues of wheat fields, the mineral gray of natural stone, or the russet colors of fall leaves. For the Japanese or Scandinavians, these understated tones have a truthfulness that connects on an innate level. The Japanese, in particular, would use in their traditional architecture a neutral clay paint textured with sand to celebrate and enhance the soft glow of natural light that would fall on a wall's surface.

Everyone will react to color in a unique way, but color psychology dictates that certain colors tend to relate to certain emotions. White, for example, has connotations with cleanliness and purity, and yellow inspires positivity, while green is connected to nature, harmony, health, and vitality. Japanese and Scandinavian design aims to create a retreat from the world. Neutral colors tend to be a classic choice, but it's precisely because of their conservatism and reliability that they make us feel safe and secure. When the world feels increasingly chaotic and overwhelming, neutral colors can help us settle our nervous system and find a sense of peace.

NEUTRAL COLOR GROUPS

A neutral color is a muted hue that appears to lack any color at all. Neutrals don't have the intensity of bolder, more saturated colors, but instead they act as a silent blank canvas to bring calm to your home. You might initially think that all creams and beiges look the same, but neutrals vary greatly in tone, tint, and temperature, making them some of the hardest colors to choose for a space. We've moved past the insipid magnolia of the 1980s and the cool grays of the 1990s to embrace a broad palette of neutrals that spans from bright whites and biscuit-toned beiges, through earthy taupes and terra-cotta, to rich ochers and chocolate browns. They can typically be grouped into four families: pure neutrals, near neutrals, warm neutrals, and cool neutrals. You can use different tones of the same color or family group to build up a scheme and create a richly layered space that has depth, harmony, and texture. For example, you might paint the walls in a pale beige then use varying shades of cinnamon and brown in your furniture and accessories to add interest. Luckily there aren't too many rules when it comes to pairing neutrals—the appeal of these tones is that they go with anything.

COLOR SYMBOLISM IN JAPANESE CULTURE

Midori (green)
This verdant hue symbolizes vitality, fertility, and growth. The Japanese have an annual Greenery Day (Midori no Hi), or public holiday.

Kuro (black)
Black is associated with formality and elegance, in addition to mourning, together with the color white.

Ao (blue)
Blue denotes dignity, stability, and security, and relates to the expanse of sea surrounding the Japanese archipelago.

Shiro (white)
The purest color in the spectrum, relating to truth and humility, as well as mourning.

Aka (red)
A national color of Japan, this bold tone represents power, protection, and prosperity. Considered auspicious, it is often used in shrines, temples, and for Japanese festivals.

Chairo (brown)
Brown relates to the earth and has connotations with durability. The Japanese word chairo means tea color, representing the enduring importance of tea in Japanese culture.

Ki (gold)
Like many other nations, gold symbolizes prestige and wealth, and is used to decorate Japanese temples and shrines.

The four pure neutrals are black, brown, white, and gray. Created by combining two complementary colors, they don't have any undertone in them. They act as a base for all neutrals and can be blended with a small amount of primary color to create any of the variations below.

Near neutrals are a toned-down version of pure neutrals and are created when you mix a primary color with a pure neutral. They're not as saturated as their pure counterparts and will appear to have a subtle undertone. You can have lighter or darker near neutrals and examples include tan, beige, and off-white.

Warm neutrals are near neutrals that have yellow, red, orange, or pink undertones. They appear sunny, earthy, or even fiery, and can be used to add visual warmth and coziness to a space.

Cool neutrals are made by mixing green, blue, or purple with a pure neutral to create colors with a little less heat. These neutrals tend to bring a fresh, crisp, and composed feel to a room.

HOW TO CHOOSE THE PERFECT NEUTRAL COLOR

Room orientation

The most important thing to consider is the direction your room faces. This will dictate the quality and tone of natural light in a space, and therefore how a color will be perceived by the eye. North-facing spaces tend to have a cooler light and can benefit from being warmed up with yellow or pink-based tones, such as beiges and ochers. For east- and west-facing rooms, think about the time of day when you are using the space—east-facing spaces get the sunlight in the morning, while west-facing spaces enjoy it in the afternoon. You can then decide if you want to embrace the warmth of the light or balance it with a cooler color. South-facing rooms are the most versatile of spaces and can handle almost any color, thanks to their abundance of strong, warm sunshine. But if your space is particularly sunny it will be able to take a blue or green-based neutral.

Undertones

When a paint color is mixed together by combining two or more colors, there will be a dominant tone that is the color you see as it comes out of the tin. But there will also be an undertone hidden within the color that will make a subtle difference to the way it appears once dry. With neutrals, this is easiest to see when you place your color sample next to a pure white background. Colors can have warm or cool undertones—a warm color will typically have red, orange, pink, or yellow undertones, while a cool color will have blue, green, or purple undertones. The temperature of a color will impact the overall ambience of your space.

Mood and feel

Take the time to think about how you will be using the room and what feeling you hope to create within it. Do you want it to feel cozy and cocooning with a richer, moodier neutral, or do you need to feel energized and uplifted with a brighter, cooler color?

Paint samples

Don't make the common mistake of painting all your samples directly onto one bit of wall—they will all start to influence the tone of each other and it can be easy to get overwhelmed with options. Instead, paint each sample onto a large piece of paper and pin onto the wall individually using masking tape. That way you can move them around the room to see how the light influences them at different times of the day.

Color drenching

Consider painting every surface of the room in the same color to create an expansive, cohesive feel in a space—including woodwork, window frames, and ceilings as well as walls. It will help give the illusion of taller ceilings because your eye won't be able to perceive where the walls stop and the ceiling begins.

Paint finish

Choose the right finish for your surface to help ensure longevity. Typically that means emulsion for walls and eggshell or gloss for woodwork. You can also get multipurpose dead flat paints that can be painted onto any surface for ease and speed.

Shape and Form

Contemporary Japanese and Scandinavian design is all about reducing things down to only what is necessary, and that includes shapes, forms, and lines. It's doing away with ornate detail and decorative complexity in favor of organic contours, clean lines, and a general sense of simplicity. This helps to create a feeling of peaceful calm, in a space where your senses aren't overwhelmed with too much visual clutter.

The Scandinavian philosophy teaches us that it is not necessary to overcomplicate something unnecessarily with extra components when you can make something just as good, if not better, with less. Classic Scandinavian furniture, for example, is known for its functionalism, seeking to reduce lines to their minimum and attempt to make chairs out of a single material or repeated element. As the famous Danish designer Hans J. Wegner once said, "Many foreigners have asked me how we created the Danish style. I've answered that it was a continuous process of purification and simplification—to cut down to the simplest possible design of four legs, a seat, and a combined back and armrest."

This process of purification extends across all elements of a Japandi interior, from straight architectural lines and empty walls to elegant furniture designs and minimalist, barely there window treatments. In Japandi-style kitchens, you won't find decorative handles on the cabinet fronts, but hidden integrated handles, if any at all. In living rooms, low-lying sideboards extend across whole walls, providing an uninterrupted line of streamlined storage. The result is unobtrusive, helping to create a sense of order and repose. While the outside world is full of distractions and jarring colors, a Japandi interior acts as a palate cleanser against all the noise.

CURVES AND ORGANIC SHAPES

A Japandi space needs some natural softness to cushion the clean lines of formal minimalism. This comes in the form of smooth curves, circles, and organic shapes. Curves can be useful from a practical point of view—we feel like we can move around them more easily and not have the danger of bumping into a sharp corner or hard edge. But more importantly, they can also bring a sense of comfort. Studies have shown that curved forms are generally seen to be more welcoming than straight lines, evoking feelings of calm and relaxation.

This might be because circular forms create natural gathering points in a room where we might settle and connect with one another, whether it's with a round dining table, a curved coffee table, or a central sculptural pendant light. Curves also have an inherently graceful quality—you feel like you can run your hand around a smooth edge of a piece of furniture, or sink into the sweeping curvature of a chair, or cradle the form of a handmade cup in your hands.

The organic shapes of Japandi spaces most significantly relate to forms and contours seen in the natural world. Perfect straight lines are rarely seen in nature. Instead you find ripples on water, whorls in an unfurling flower, or concentric circles in the grain of a tree trunk. Japanese Zen gardens, for example, use asymmetry and curved forms to emulate nature and create spaces for contemplation. The raked patterns in the gravel represent the movement of water, offering a sense of serenity, while sweeping paths guide you through a space, drawing you to certain meditative moments in the garden. We can use the same concept in our interiors, using curved forms to lead the eye into a space and create restful accents that help lift an otherwise uniform interior.

CLEAN LINES

Both Scandinavian and Japanese interiors rely on clean lines to bring as few interruptions as possible. Traditional Japanese homes tended to minimize the amount of everydat stuff, instead preferring to highlight the more ethereal qualities of a space, such as the quiet beauty of natural light or the texture of organic materials. The architectural form of Japanese wooden frame houses typically prioritizes uninterrupted views outside and a connection to nature, as well as a modular construction system that standardizes the proportions of rooms and creates a series of flexible spaces that can be opened or closed off with sliding doors and partitions. Low-lying furniture further cements this idea of reduction and refinement, creating a very particular spatial quality that feels airy and expansive. Straight lines dominate and also help frame views through rooms.

The Scandinavians, on the other hand, spearheaded the idea of functionalism in architecture and design during the early 20th century as another facet of modernism. Functionalism responded to the need for purpose-built urban housing after the First and Second World Wars, while rejecting the ornamentation of the past. Architects like Arne Jacobsen, Alvar Aalto, and Vilhelm Lauritzen used clean lines to emphasize the function and purpose of a space. Homes would typically feature flat roofs, expansive architectural glazing, naturally lit rooms, and a feeling of free-flowing space.

Japandi interiors blend the clean, functionalist minimalism of Scandinavian design with the meticulous order and purity of Japanese design. While both regions had quite different approaches, they are united in their desire to balance form and function.

Opposites Attract

The key to the serenity of Japandi interiors is in the delicate balance between contrasting elements. Inspired by the ancient Chinese concept of yin and yang, there is a duality between complementary opposites, such as light and dark, the masculine and feminine, hard and soft, and stillness and movement. It makes sense that you can't have one without the other. The beauty is in appreciating the play between contrasts so as to create a space that is more than the sum of its parts. A sense of harmony comes from a feeling of equality between elements, shapes, and forms, where each is allowed to shine.

Represented as two interconnecting halves of a circle, the concept of yin and yang, or yin-yang, originates in ancient Chinese philosophy but has deep roots in Eastern thought more generally. The idea depicts the harmony that is found between different energies. It was brought over to Japan in the 5th and 6th centuries, along with the idea that there are five key elements that are the driving force behind life. These are: earth, fire, wood, water, and metal. Everything in the natural world essentially comes back to these elements.

Inyo is the Japanese equivalent of yin-yang and is shown as a red circle inside a white circle, drawing parallels to the national Japanese flag. *In* (or *yin* in Chinese) symbolizes the feminine and can be seen as passive, dark, and negative, while *yo* (or *yang* in Chinese) is masculine, light, and positive. The two elements coexist and are held together as one yet are distinctly separate. In Japanese culture, *inyo* has influenced everything from meditation practices and superstitions to artwork and interiors.

We can take inspiration from *inyo* or yin-yang to create balance and moments of beauty in our homes. It's about celebrating each element on its own merit, but also making sure that everything ties together into a harmonious whole. This could be expressed by paying as much attention to the negative space around objects as the objects themselves. For example, if you had a piece of art on your walls, you would want to give it room to breathe and not add clutter around it that might distract from its beauty. It's about taking a thoughtful approach to how and where you might place the detail in an interior.

NATURAL CONTRASTS

Masculine and feminine

Masculine elements in interior design can be loosely depicted with dark, cool colors, straight lines, and hard edges, whereas the feminine is thought to be expressed with curved forms, soft textures, and detailed patterns.

Light and shadow

While Scandinavian design seeks to maximize the limited light in the winter months, Japanese design embraces the idea of dimness and shadow known as *kage*. In traditional Japanese architecture, *shoji* screens—room dividers made of paper panels—are used to diffuse and filter natural light from the sides of a building. The gentle quality of the light takes on a poetic beauty, while shadows infuse a space with atmosphere. We can use that idea in our homes by carefully thinking about the use and placement of light fittings, to transform the space from day to night. Instead of just one central pendant light, try to create cozy little pockets of light around your home with plenty of table and floor lamps.

Hard and soft

Hard elements are the solid, architectural features in a space, such as glass doors, walls, stone floors, or wooden joinery. Soft elements are the upholstery, textiles, rugs, and accessories. A space with a lot of hard surfaces and clean, straight lines needs the softness that comes from lighter fabrics and materials to help it feel homey and like somewhere you can genuinely relax in.

Smooth and rough

Having a careful play between smooth surfaces and rough textures can help prevent a space from looking flat or boring. A space will look much more visually exciting if there is a contrast between different materials, such as a tactile wooden coffee table paired with a plain linen sofa or a coarse jute rug next to smooth wooden flooring.

Warm and cold

When we talk about heat and cold in interiors, we don't just mean the ambient temperature of a room, but the feeling of warmth or chill that comes from colors, tones, and textures. A space that has too many cool tones, such as blues and grays, might feel stark or unwelcoming, but if you introduce some warmer tones you can make the space feel more natural and less one-dimensional. Even natural wood can add warmth to a room.

Stillness and movement

It helps to give a space fluidity and energy if there is a balance between moments of serenity and moments of life. Plants, branches, and floral arrangements can bring movement to a space of otherwise fixed, static objects, as can natural light filtering through sheer curtains or the accent of a graphic pattern.

Giving Life to Flowers

Ikebana is the ancient Japanese art of arranging flowers. The term literally translates as "giving life to flowers," combining the Japanese words *ikeru*—to "arrange flowers, have life, and be living"—and *hana*, meaning "flower." *Ikebana* is about finding beauty in nature and using emotion, meaning, and intuition to create a graceful, balanced arrangement of seasonal stems, branches, and leaves. When viewed in an interior, they invite us to stop and pause for a moment.

The art of *ikebana* is as much about the process of creation as it is about the composition. The Japanese see *ikebana* as a respected ritual, one that requires time and reflection to help deepen our connection with nature. Every step of the process is deliberate to the point where it almost becomes a form of meditation, leading to a greater sense of self-awareness and contentment.

One of the three Japanese arts of refinement, *ikebana* dates back to the 8th century. It was first born out of the floral offerings that were left by Buddhist monks. Later it was used by Japanese generals to calm their minds and aid decision making. The art form traditionally follows a set of established rules that govern the practice and composition of arrangements. In Japan, there are different schools of thought, each with their own distinctive philosophy and style. Beginners can gain a certificate in as little as three months, but it can take years to fully train and become a true master. Some of the more avant-garde schools are more open to the freedom of creative expression, believing that *ikebana* can be enjoyed "anytime, anywhere, and by anyone." To give it a go, you'll first need a flower frog with brass needles (called a *kenzan*) to help hold your stems in place. The result should have a subtle, quiet beauty, as if a snapshot of nature has been frozen in time.

THE KEY PRINCIPLES OF *IKEBANA*

Seasonality

Flowers are typically arranged in different formations, depending on the time of year. In the summer, for example, you might see shallower vessels with more water to give a feeling of freshness. What's really important is choosing stems and floral varieties that are in season.

Minimalism

Less is more when it comes to *ikebana*, you only need a few choice stems and branches. Consider the negative space between items as much as the pieces themselves. Don't overcrowd the arrangement but let each stem sing.

Color

As well as creating a balanced composition of different-sized stems, you also should aim to have a harmonious color palette. The colors of some flowers are considered unlucky in Japan, while others are a bit more auspicious. Red tends to be associated with fires, for example, and red flowers are typically used at funerals. If you were to offer a housewarming gift in Japan, you might use white flowers as they symbolize water that could put out a fire, a long-standing concern as Japanese houses were traditionally made entirely of wood. Bright color isn't completely off the table when it comes to *ikebana*, but it's just used in a more selective way, for example with just one or two buds. The color of the vase tends to be more neutral so as not to deflect too much from the flowers. Typically the Japanese use the color bronze to reflect the earth.

Asymmetry

On the whole the Japanese believe that odd numbers are more appealing than even numbers. This is likely because you never see perfect, equal forms in nature. Groups of threes or fives naturally look more pleasing to the eye than something more formal. More traditional arrangements are based on a triangle with three main points set at different heights, representing heaven, earth, and human.

Balance

Ikebana often balances the yin to the yang so there is a harmony between opposites and duality of meaning.

Time

Ikebana was based on the Buddhist mentality of preserving life, dictating everything from the shape of the vase to the ways in which the flowers could last longer. Traditionally you should always be able to see the water in the vessel, to represent the stems coming out of the ground. Also consider choosingw closed buds so that you can watch them open and enjoy them for as long as possible.

Emotion and meaning

Hanakotoba is the Japanese language of flowers that is used to convey emotion without the need for words. In *ikebana*, plants have coded meanings and masters use symbolism to create evocative arrangements.

Poetic Modernism

AN INTERVIEW WITH SIGNE BINDSLEV HENRIKSEN
AND PETER BUNDGAARD RÜTZOU, FOUNDERS OF SPACE COPENHAGEN

Founded in 2005 by Signe Bindslev Henriksen and Peter Bundgaard Rützou, Space Copenhagen is a Danish design studio that has created interior projects across the world, from the first Noma in Copenhagen to the 11 Howard hotel in New York, and more recently, Hotel Toranomon Hills in Tokyo. From private homes to hotels, and across furniture and lighting design, they take a slow, intuitive approach to design that prioritizes tactility, quality, and longevity, as well as a curiosity around the emotional perception of interior spaces. Here Signe and Peter talk about how the introspective nature of Japanese design has influenced their practice, which they have come to define as "poetic modernism."

Can you describe your approach to design and what you mean by poetic modernism?

PETER: We were educated in the Scandinavian tradition and were interested in minimalism. There was a sense of purity and a celebration of emptiness that links slightly to some Japanese terms. But we came to realize that there was a lack of connectivity between whoever enters the space and the space itself. There is another side to the story, which isn't as pragmatic. It has a more fragile, emotional side, which means that whenever we encounter a space, we feel something. And we understand it primarily by intuition. Sometimes the most precise language for intuition is not a very descriptive set of words, but a metaphorical language that enables you to express an emotion. It's the juxtaposition of those two perspectives—the functional and the emotional—that creates a tension we try to relate to.

SIGNE: Somehow it also relates very strongly to our interest in Asia and especially Japanese architecture. It links to traditional aspects of tea-house architecture as a very precise exercise in ritual and function, but there are also soft values, such as the idea of *wabi sabi*, and the essence of patination and texture.

How do you look to create harmony and balance in an interior space?

PETER: There is a famous Japanese book called *In Praise of Shadows* by Jun'ichirō Tanizaki. What it proposes is something that I think for most people is a surprise. It's not about prioritizing the light, but appreciating the shadow. By doing so, you create depth and mystery. We try to create this sense of duality between hard and soft, feminine and masculine, light and shadow. It's always trying to counterbalance a choice, so you have an element of contrast.

What commonalities have you found between your Nordic values and Japanese design values?

SIGNE: I think there are definitely a lot. I think we're both committed to certain base values, such as an interest in organic materials, craft, and the aging of those materials, as well as a kind of quietness and very ascetic way of being in the world. We both have a lifestyle and a language that is not too pretentious.

PETER: I think from our latitude, the weather has been extremely significant. If you look back, the reality of the Scandinavian lifestyle was that it was very tough, and we didn't have a lot of resources. So the appreciation of doing something with what you've got is something fundamentally anchored in the Scandinavian lifestyle. We still take that into account—that desire to filter things down—even though we don't need to do it anymore, because it reflects our perception of how we see the world.

How has Japanese design influenced your practice and the projects you create?

SIGNE: I think what we're incredibly drawn to in the Japanese aesthetic is that it has this very rare combination of catching your attention at the same time as pointing to something inside you. It opens the possibility of you diving a little bit inward.

PETER: I think there's another interesting aspect that points to how we're different and how we each treat our legacies. In Scandinavia, our back catalog of references within our own culture is not sacred. We appreciate them, but we can also see that they can be open to interpretation or change. But when you look at traditional Japanese architecture, there are certain patterns or structures that you cannot remove from one context to another. And they feel very challenged if you say, why or why not? But not allowing for change is also somehow the secret of Japan's excellent craft tradition because they practice repetition to absurd degrees, which allows them to do things no one else can do.

How did you first come to work in Japan?

PETER: We actually started traveling to Japan long before we had any work there. Then we started working internationally and one of the big families there, the Mori Building Company, spotted us and that opened up things for our first collaboration. The thing with working in Japan is that it's very slow moving. It takes about twice as long as it does everywhere else, which has to do with a very meticulous way of working.

SIGNE: While I was studying, I also went to Japan to learn about wooden joints, which was a huge interest of mine at that time. I ended up working in an architecture office for five months. It was an introduction into something that was so completely different and foreign in a very positive way. We've always been looking for a way to engage with Japan one way or another. We feel somehow very related and feel that there's some kind of strange feedback system between our two countries, even though we're so incredibly different.

PETER: We should emphasize that Japan is still a mystery. It's as if there's this layering, once you think you understand, then something opens up and then all of a sudden you question things again.

What have you learned from working in Japan?

SIGNE: Coming from a small country it creates a natural curiosity toward something else, which is bigger and not necessarily easy to interpret from first glance. That's one thing we can see from all the amazing architects and designers that have come out of Scandinavia—they were all traveling and seeking inspiration. We've always been seeking out ideas.

PETER: You could say the Nordics are extroverts. And the Japanese have been looking inward; for centuries they didn't look for anything outside their own country.

Why do you think Japandi interiors are particularly appealing right now?

SIGNE: I think it's definitely linking up to our new religion in the Western countries, which replaces a lot of other values that kept society together many years ago. This new lifestyle that treasures healthy values and the balance between the mind and body. Even though there might be a fascination with minimalism in general, I think the reason why there is a huge wave of fascination for so many people is because it relates to some of the things they are trying to incorporate into their own lives.

PETER: You could say there is a loss of faith at the moment. There is this existential sort of loss of direction. We look for other means of understanding and creating a sense of compass. And it relates to nature. It relates to something that when we reach back to our original story, we find it very easy to put some degree of trust into. And that's very well anchored in both traditional Japanese architecture and the Nordic tradition, and our endless fascination with natural materials.

SIGNE: This soft and mild way of being in the world just feels right at the moment.

SUSTAINABLE LIVING

It can be said that the Japanese and Scandinavian approaches to design are inherently sustainable and enduring in appeal. Both philosophies have long held a profound respect for nature, seeking to create a harmonious balance between what we take from the world and what we create. Today, the Japandi style offers a compelling alternative to consumerism and modern materialistic values, prioritizing quality, locality, eco-friendly materials, and a mindful way of living.

With design principles rooted in honesty and simplicity, these two philosophies epitomize the reduce, reuse, recycle motto. In a world where you can buy something new at a click of a button and have it shipped across the world, the Japandi approach instead places a high value on longevity and durability over trend-led fads.

This sustainable way of living ties in with the Swedish concept of lagom, or "not too little, not too much." Lagom is about seeking a more balanced life with just enough of what we need, whether that refers to how many possessions we own or the amount of energy we use. Lagom is not so much about scarcity, but being aware of a shared, collective responsibility where everyone benefits if we all live a life in moderation. We consume not just the right amount for ourselves but also for the planet so we can all live in synergy. Living lagom is being respectful of the resources we take and not getting carried away by consumerism.

Quality and Craftsmanship

Both the Japanese and Scandinavian design movements
are renowned around the world for their dedication to expert
craftsmanship. With an uncompromising attention to detail,
each region prides itself on the design of high-quality furniture
that has been finessed by hand and made with the very best
materials. The appeal of these thoughtfully made objects is that
if something is made to last, it won't need to be replaced and
can go on being enjoyed for years, even decades, to come.

There are certain Scandinavian design classics that have stood the test of time
and are instantly recognizable—take for instance, Hans J. Wegner's Wishbone
chair or Arne Jacobsen's Egg chair. Even though they were designed nearly
seventy-five years ago, they still look as fresh and relevant as the year they were
released. Time has added value and a renewed appreciation for the story behind
the design. Why do they have such enduring appeal? Because each designer
reduced the design down to something that was pure, simple, and functional.
Yet they could only do that because of the specialist carpentry skills that had
been honed by experienced craftspeople in the years before. The Scandinavian
design heritage is based on a legacy of constantly reinventing and refining
modern design. As with Japanese design, there is a sense of respect for the
person who made a particular object, and a desire to preserve the skills of the
maker so that they can be passed down. This adds much more value—and we're
not just talking about monetary value—to a product than if it had been mass
produced. It is the care that goes into the making process that adds worth,
as well as beauty.

Japan and Scandinavia have a long history of sharing these skills and learning from one another. It was a mutually beneficial collaboration: Japan needed to create new products to export, and with a culture of living on the floor, had never really had to focus on the making of chairs before; while Scandinavia had a curiosity for a country that was previously shut off from the world. This longstanding relationship could be seen in a series of "Good Design" exhibitions that were hosted in Japanese department stores in the 1950s and '60s, presenting designs for the first time by Alvar Aalto, Finn Juhl, and Børge Mogensen, among others, to a Japanese audience that was hungry for the modern Western aesthetic. This culture continues today with design collaborations that combine the Nordic design heritage with Japanese form and craftsmanship. Sometimes it's even hard to distinguish between the influences, such is the fusion now of the two design ideals.

JAPANESE CRAFTSMANSHIP

In Japanese culture, craftsmanship is part of the everyday experience—it's in the ceramics people drink their tea out of, the handcrafted paper they write on, and the spaces they inhabit. Unlike the West, there is no hierarchy between different art forms and crafts, such as pottery, furniture making, and architecture. Each has its place, and a piece of craft is valued as much for the techniques that define it, as the pleasure someone might get from using it. In that sense, design is egalitarian.

The Japanese equivalent for the word craftsmanship is *monozukuri,* yet like many Japanese words, it proves hard to define and goes further than what the West might simply describe as manufacturing. *Monozukuri* means "the making of things" but it also describes the relentless dedication that the Japanese have for perfecting their craft. As such, it recognizes the hard work of the maker. When it comes to craftsmanship, the Japanese seem to have an unparalleled patience for design and nothing is too much effort if it brings out the best of a material. In Japan, there are, for example, over 400 different wooden joints, which have traditionally been used to build homes and furniture and are based on thousands of years of carpentry experience. With a desire not to be wasteful, many don't utilize glue or nails. Wooden joinery is mostly revered for the extensive training and knowledge that goes into the design of a piece. The aim is always to highlight the natural beauty of a material and ornamentation is typically seen as vulgar. Japanese craftsmanship is therefore defined by simple forms, straight lines, and plain, unfinished wooden surfaces.

SCANDINAVIAN CRAFTSMANSHIP

The Scandinavian design tradition is defined by a strong social purpose. Scandinavian designers, especially those coming out of Denmark, sought to create furniture and spaces that would improve people's daily lives. They recognized a need for useful objects that would marry both form and function. A chair had to be comfortable and ergonomic as well as beautiful. In a similar approach to Japan where design is everywhere and in everything, Scandinavia sought to democratize design and make it accessible to all, whether that was with designs that could be mass produced or with more affordable flat-packed furniture.

With an abundance of wood at their disposal, Scandinavian designers developed a deep understanding of the material. After the Second World War they had to become economical with designs when materials became more scarce. Think of modern Scandinavian furniture and you likely picture slender wooden forms, tapered legs, and light, airy pieces. A lot of Danish modernist furniture designers understood joint details and how to refine the handmade because of their background in cabinet making (see page 69).

Before putting something into production, they would typically showcase their prototypes at cabinetmakers' fairs, such as those founded by the Copenhagen Cabinetmakers' Guild in 1927 to help promote the value of traditional craft. A lot of the Danish modern designs from that era are still in continuous production today and Scandinavian brands continue to reissue forgotten design classics from the archive.

Eco-friendly Materials

In Japanese and Scandinavian design, natural materials aren't just chosen for their texture and aesthetic qualities, but because these materials typically have a lower environmental impact. Often they're renewable, easily recyclable, biodegradable, and intrinsically durable in nature. But that doesn't mean we shouldn't be mindful of what we use. With the pressure on finite raw materials, there is now a need to invest in ever more sustainable alternatives, such as recycled materials and waste products, that make use of what we've already got.

With Japandi interiors, there is often a desire to trace materials back to their source and have some level of accountability for where something has come from and what resources were used in the process. Locally sourced materials are favored over unusual products from far-flung locations, helping to root spaces in their immediate context and surroundings, and reduce emissions. Japan, in particular, has a heritage of using native timber going back centuries and supporting reforestation projects to keep them in good supply. If you're a conscious consumer today, you'll likely want to know not only where a piece of design was made, and who made it, but also where the material was grown or created. For example, some hardwoods can be illegally sourced and contribute to the destruction and deforestation of tropical rainforests. Most companies are now expected to have an environmental report or statement on their website, and some even have a life-cycle analysis for each product or calculations for CO_2 emissions.

There are also globally recognized and trusted certification standards that help consumers know how sustainable a piece of furniture is. Across the world, the FSC label from the Forest Stewardship Council is used to indicate if timber has been responsibly sourced. It's a standard that helps track the wood from FSC-certified forests to the consumer, making sure the production process is socially beneficial and environmentally viable. Global Organic Textile Standard (GOTS) is a similar standard for organic fibers, while Oeko-Tex™ offers verification for organic cotton. Consumers will no doubt demand for more transparency in the future.

While Japanese and Scandinavian design has relied on natural materials thus far, there is also an awareness of the need for more circularity in the design industry. Circular design is a zero-waste movement that creates materials or products that can be reused, recycled, or repaired, with the aim of conserving resources, reducing waste, and protecting nature. Instead of constantly creating new designs in virgin materials, the idea is that we might, for example, be able to disassemble and easily replace a part of a chair that was broken, use offcuts from the manufacturing process to make other designs, or use discarded waste to create new materials. By creating a closed-loop system, we can reduce the amount we send to landfill and extend the life of what we already own. We can also practice this approach in our homes by upcycling furniture, fixing broken objects, and making more conscious choices.

MATERIAL POSSIBILITIES

Hemp

Hemp is one of nature's most durable and versatile fibers. The renewable crop grows rapidly, and requires minimal water and no pesticides or fertilizers. Looking for a more responsible alternative to the plastic shell chair, designers Foersom & Hiort-Lorenzen spent two decades testing and prototyping before releasing the Mat chair, made of hemp fibers and eelgrass, with Danish brand Normann Copenhagen in 2024. These hemp chairs have more than 200 percent less environmental impact than their polypropylene counterparts.

Algae

Algae-based polymers and composites could be another viable replacement for plastic. Microalgae, microorganisms that are invisible to the human eye, have already been used to create bio-bricks and algae-based cement. In 2022, experimental Copenhagen-based Natural Material Studio created a seaweed fabric dyed with spirulina algae that can be used to make curtains and clothing.

Mycelium

Mycelium is the underground structure of thin roots that form the base of a fungus. It is quick and low cost to grow in soil or agricultural waste, is 100 percent biodegradable, and is stronger than concrete relative to its weight. Mycelium can be processed and molded to form everything from biodegradable packaging to pendant lights.

Ocean waste plastic

In 2019, Danish brand Mater brought a 1955 chair design by Nanna Ditzel into the future by reproducing the originally wooden design in recycled ocean waste plastic. They collaborated with Letbek and Plastix, which upcycles fishnet waste, to create the Ocean outdoor collection, consisting of a chair, bench, and table set. Mater estimates that each Ocean product saves 82 percent of CO_2 emissions compared to virgin equivalents.

Coffee grounds

Mater has also found a way to make furniture out of discarded coffee bean shells as well as sawdust waste. The patented material Matek combines these waste materials with a binder to create a compound that can be press molded. Mater used the material to reimagine the classic School chair (1958) by Danish modernists Børge Mogensen and Esben Klint.

Cellulose

Cellulose residue from cardboard and paper production creates an estimated seven millions tons of waste per year globally. Cellulose fibers have typically been used in the fashion industry to create plant-based textiles, but waste cellulose has potential for use in furniture and construction materials.

Flax

Flax fibers come from the stem of the flax plant. It is lightweight yet stronger than cotton. The fibers are typically used to make linen fabrics, as well as paper and even bank notes. In 2017, Japanese designer Jin Kuramoto used flax fibers to create the Jin chair for Swedish furniture brand Offecct, shaping thin layers of flax fibers on top of each other to create a strong shell.

Mindful Consumption

In an age of abundance and excess, the Japandi way of living frames itself in direct opposition to consumerism and materialistic ideals. It takes a more intentional point of view that encourages us to reflect on our choices so we can practice more sustainable lifestyles. Instead of discarding our possessions when they no longer serve us, or automatically buying something new, we can remember the three enduring Rs: reduce, reuse, and recycle.

REDUCE

To start to make the changes toward a more sustainable way of living, we first need to reframe our thinking around how we decorate our homes and curate our lifestyles. It can be hard to know where to begin and we can easily start to feel a bit helpless if we worry that our individual actions won't add up to make a big difference. We can start by simply buying less. If you have fewer possessions, you're already doing something to create less waste. In the past, our parents and grandparents would have perhaps redecorated their homes every ten to fifteen years, maybe even more. They might have inherited heirloom furniture or kept the same dining table for their entire lifetime. Today, we treat interiors like fast fashion. The media encourages us to make over our homes every season and constantly buy new object after new object.

Try to be wary of fashions that might come and go, or falling into the trap of buying something just because everyone else has it. It's easy to be seduced by a trend without truly considering if it's right for your home and then be left with an item that you don't know what to do with. If you do find yourself tempted by a new piece of homeware, resist impulse buys and choose items because they mean something to you. Take a moment to slow down and remember your values.

Ask yourself if you have something like it already and consider stepping away to reflect on the purchase—if you're still thinking about it after twenty-four hours, it might be worth going back. Invest in quality over quantity, then you're less likely to keep needing to buy new things because the things you do buy will last longer and better serve their purpose.

REUSE

If we take the time to look after what we've already got, our existing possessions and precious resources can go on being used over and over again. This includes second-hand furniture—mixing old and new helps add character to a space and pre-loved design is a great way to stylishly decorate your home while also being mindful of the environment. Vintage buys can often be more affordable than new, yet they tend to hold their value better in the long term. You also know you're getting something completely unique that no one else might have.

In today's society we tend to think that items are replaceable and we can just buy something better, or newer, or shinier. But repairing items that are broken or worn can help you fall in love with them again. It could mean reupholstering an old sofa or securing a wobbly leg on a chair.

Look after your things and keep them lasting for longer by giving them a bit of TLC; for instance, re-oiling the surface of a dining table, touching up paintwork, or cleaning and airing a rug. You'll be less likely to want to replace them if they're in good condition, and if you do, you know they will be valued and go to a good home.

RECYCLE

We can look beyond appearances and use our creativity to ensure that old items can be utilized again in alternative forms, beyond what they were first conceived for. A great way to do this is with upcycling, which involves repurposing and modifying an existing object with the intention of giving it greater value. Turn an old piece of furniture into a rewarding creative project by giving it a lick of paint or adding some new handles. Use fabric off-cuts to make patchwork cushions or turn a vintage chest of drawers into a bathroom vanity. You could even try making your own piece of abstract art by painting over an old canvas with textured paint or creating homemade candles by filling old vessels and vintage glasses with wax.

If you do need to let something go, allow someone else to find joy in your unloved possessions by passing them on. Consider donating to a nearby thrift store, selling your homeware at a flea market, or finding a local recycling service.

Reframing Waste

Sustainable living needn't be costly or just reserved for the well off. There are small steps everyone can take to improve their environmental footprint and reduce waste, both inside the home and further afield. Part of that is about finding a renewed joy in what we already own and reframing how we value our already limited resources.

The Japanese have a concept called *mottainai*, which expresses a feeling of regret or sadness when something goes to waste. According to the Japanese dictionary *Kōjien*, the disapproving phrase is used when the value of an item or object is not put to good use. It is thought to have stemmed from ancient Buddhist philosophy and the idea that everything is connected—or in other words, our objects and possessions exist only in relationship to ourselves and others. We give things meaning, so it is our responsibility to appreciate and honor the things around us, including what nature gives us. If we waste something, it then becomes meaningless. In English, *mottainai* more directly translates as "Don't be wasteful!" or the traditional saying "Waste not, want not." It might be used in Japan if someone leaves something on their plate after a meal, discards litter on the street, or needlessly throws away something that could still be used.

More recently the term *mottainai* has been used by environmentalists to encourage people to turn the tide on a throwaway culture. The *mottainai* campaign, launched in 2005 in Japan, seeks to add a fourth "R" of "Respect" to the three R's and promote a feeling of reverence toward our global resources and the environment. It was championed by Wangari Maathai, the late Kenyan political activist who founded the Green Belt Movement and went on to become the first African woman to win the Nobel Peace Prize in 2004. She took the idea to a global audience at the United Nations Climate Change Conference in

2009, urging the world to "express gratitude, to respect and avoid wastage." For Maathai, *mottainai* was about respecting the things we use every day and treating what we own with care.

Now the spirit of *mottainai* is spread through Japan with special *mottainai* flea markets and handmade craft fairs. There's even children-only markets to encourage the next generation to understand the value of money, as well as dedicated toy hospitals where volunteers will repair broken toys for free. As we have already seen with the Japanese art of *kintsugi* on page 80, and decluttering on page 54, it is a very Japanese sentiment to want to seek out the hidden worth in our objects, no matter if they're broken or ugly. They would say that if we can find the joy in fixing things or passing things on, we might find a better sense of gratitude or fulfillment in the process.

REUSABLE FUROSHIKI

Furoshiki are traditional Japanese wrapping cloths that are typically used as reusable alternatives to single-use wrapping paper and throwaway plastic bags. Historically they were used to carry a person's belongings to the bathhouse and protect their kimono while bathing—*furo* translates as "bath," and *shiki* as "spread." Today they have found renewed popularity around the world with eco-conscious consumers. Typically beautifully patterned with intricate designs, the fabric wraps can be tied and folded to thoughtfully present gifts, protect books, or transport food and bento boxes. In an effort to promote their use, the Japanese government has suggested fourteen official patterns with different knots and ties to carry everything from a heavy watermelon to a water bottle. If you've received something wrapped in *furoshiki*, it is customary to return the wrap to the person who gave it to you.

HOW TO REFRESH YOUR HOME FOR FREE

Rearrange the furniture

Shifting things around in a room can bring a renewed energy to a space. If you live in a smaller home with fewer possibilities for reconfiguration, it could be as simple as swapping your accessories from room to room or restyling your shelves in a different arrangement.

Shop from your home

We all have much more in our homes than we think, and sometimes we just need to see our possessions from a new perspective. A piece of art might give a completely different feel to a space when placed in a different corner. If you have a lot of objects, gather them together into a prop stylist's cupboard or display cabinet, and then you can shop from it anytime you choose.

Style with the seasons

Take inspiration from the changing seasons and adapt your home according to the mood of nature. Store items away when you don't need them and have a rotation on the go. You might have a set of cozy blankets and throws you only bring out in winter, for example.

Find new uses for things

If something has served its purpose in one area of your home, it might be time to reimagine a different use for it, for example when you've burnt through a candle, you might use the vessel as a pen pot or miniature vase.

Bring the outside in

Go foraging in nature and freshen up your home with a sculptural branch that will last far longer than any fresh flowers.

Use leftover paint and sample pots

Get creative and use leftover paint to decorate picture frames, personalize plant pots, or upcycle a small piece of furniture to give it a fresh new look.

Source affordable art

Instead of buying a brand new print or expensive artwork, there's plenty of easy ways to create a beautiful display from nothing. For example, you could frame a page from a design magazine, a postcard from an exhibition you enjoyed, or even a child's artwork.

Host a homeware swap

This is a clothes swap, but for all your unwanted homeware that is too good to throw out. Gather your friends and ask them each to bring a couple of items to exchange: examples include vases, small objects, cookbooks, magazines, or even plant cuttings that can be propagated to make new plants.

Crowdsource

Look to websites like Freecycle and Facebook Marketplace to find valuable items that other people want to get rid of quickly. One person's trash is another person's treasure and you never know what you might find.

Honest Design

AN INTERVIEW WITH KEIJI ASHIZAWA

Based in Tokyo, Keiji Ashizawa founded his architecture and design practice Keiji Ashizawa Design in 2005. With an approach described as "honest design," the practice is known for the total design of spaces, helping to unify everything from the structure and interiors right down to bespoke furniture and landscaping. Sharing a mutual love for material richness and timeless craftsmanship, Keiji Ashizawa has collaborated with Copenhagen-based practice Norm Architects (see interview, pages 60–63) on a number of projects for Japanese furniture manufacturer Karimoku. Here Keiji discusses the design heritage that connects Japan and Scandinavia.

How would you describe your approach to architecture and design?

I describe my approach as honest design. It's not so much a concept, but a subject I have to keep thinking about and coming back to. As an architect or designer, when you design something, there's so many demands that come from the client or the maker or even from the public. Of course you must respond to their needs, and any good design has to be functional and long-lasting. But at the same time, a designer also has to respond to societal conditions, or the history or context of a place. We have to place ourselves in between these needs and judge what might be a good solution for that particular setting.

Is that also about understanding how the user experiences the space?

Yes, that's part of honest design. An architect should have some historical knowledge in order to make good architecture. I've learnt from my own experience, for instance. My understanding of a project is skewed more by society and the public than the exact client. For example, if I designed a chair, the chair should be useful for many people. The maker also has to sell a lot otherwise they cannot make a business out of it. As architects we have to think about a long period of history, maybe further back than what we've experienced in our lifetime. I believe we have to shift our thinking. I want to be very honest when I'm designing something, so I know it's coming not from a trend or the client's strong demands, but a more authentic place.

Does that honesty also relate to materials and craftsmanship?

Yes, of course. A material should be expressed as it is. If we use good materials we can use something for a long time and create a deeper connection with that object or piece of furniture. Then it will also feel nice and be comfortable for people to touch.

How has traditional Japanese design influenced that way of thinking about context and natural materials?

In traditional Japanese architecture you have sliding doors or tatami mats that you can move to another house. There's flexibility and longevity built into the design. It's like we created our very own sustainable system before we even made or added anything. I think that's still a very nice idea and we can learn a lot from the functional details you find in an old Japanese room. The other thing about Japanese architecture, especially the old wooden buildings, is that the structure is really beautiful and also quite sustainable. Every part is recyclable or changeable.

Do you think Japanese design is inherently sustainable?

Yes, completely sustainable because it's so long-lasting. We rarely throw things away. For example, we can take a tatami mat to the tatami shop and change the surface every five years. We can keep the sliding doors for more than 100 years. The sliding door in Japan has a very simple detail; we don't have any metal parts. A metal part might last maybe 15 years, but by using just one material (wood) we can use a door for 200 or 300 years. It's everlasting and I think that's really amazing. In Japan, paper can last 300 years, which is unbelievable. Now is a good time to go back to such a sustainable system.

How do you balance the functional aspects with the more poetic qualities of a space?

That's a good question. Japanese rooms are made completely from natural materials We use a lot of wood, tatami that is made of rice straw, and paper from the *mitsumata* shrub or mulberry bush. They each have a different surface and color, and the combination of materials creates a play between lightness and heaviness. It's been the historical way of doing things, but even now we are careful to create balance. It's like when you eat some nice Japanese food, every dish is a bit varied, but they complement each other. The senses become quite connected. It's the same when we design a space and specify materials: there are very subtle differences that highlight the qualities of those materials, for example, the texture. Somehow we understand how to create comfort by mixing color and materiality.

Have you taken any inspiration from Scandinavian design?

Yes, I feel the similarity with Scandinavia, especially how to use and take care of a material, and finesse the craftsmanship of a design. For example, their wooden furniture is very detailed but also quite functional. I've stayed with friends in Denmark and you can always find their grandparents' furniture, so the Scandinavians really understood how to make good, long-lasting furniture that they can keep using. They really appreciate their heritage. And even in new designs, there is some detail that is connected back to the Danish modernist tradition.

What was it like working with Norm Architects on the case study projects for Karimoku Case Study?

We were first involved in the same project for a Japanese furniture maker called Ariake. They invited a group of Scandinavian designers, including Anderssen & Voll, Norm Architects, and Note Design Studio, to visit and stay for a week in their factory in Morodomi, Japan. There was also Gabriel Tan from Singapore and Shin Azumi from Japan. We designed the furniture in the factory and discussed ideas. We realized that Norm Architects and my studio shared a very close connection. We don't want to just design the architecture, we really want to manage the whole space and create a complete concept.

We decided we wanted to work together, then Karimoku, the biggest furniture company in Japan, contacted me and I introduced them to Norm Architects. Karimoku really wanted to reach the international market. Norm Architects and I opened the gate for Karimoku to connect with the world. Karimoku has a beautiful way of making furniture where a design is made for a particular architecture project before being put into production. Every space needs furniture, obviously, so then the furniture becomes a seamless part of the space. Our first project together was Kinuta Terrace, an apartment block in Tokyo in 2019, and since then we have designed a hotel and café. We really enjoyed the exchange of culture. Not many Japanese companies have worked with Scandinavian designers, but now it's becoming more of a standard because Japanese furniture companies are highly skilled and they value the Scandinavian approach. Also in the Japanese market, many customers are really drawn to Scandinavian furniture, so they have a big opportunity here too.

What have you learned from the Scandinavian approach to design?

Scandinavian designers have very strong principles when it comes to designing furniture. They continually try to improve designs, and they know how to balance the old with the new. I felt I could learn a lot from their attitude to heritage. The Scandinavians also understand detail. The craft culture in Japan is also very strong and we still have amazing craftspeople. I hope we can keep those traditions alive.

FUNCTIONALITY

Both Japanese and Scandinavian design put function first, often before anything else. So much so that an object or interior can't be deemed truly beautiful if it is not in some way useful. Functionality prioritizes the user's experience, creating hard-working homes that work on a practical as well as stylish level.

While the Japandi aesthetic has a poetic or ephemeral quality that embraces texture and tactility, it's also deeply rooted in the functional. It is function that supports a home in being the best that it can be. It's common to feel stressed by your home when it's not meeting your needs or frustrated that you have nowhere to put anything. A functional home should be comfortable, and easy and intuitive to use, where all our storage needs are met, and there's an efficient use of the space available.

To have functionality, you need to first consider the purpose of a space. With Japanese and Scandinavian design, every design choice must have a reason. To make a home truly work for you, before even considering how it looks, it can help to make a list of every activity you want to do in each space, no matter how small or insignificant. You can then consider practical ways to integrate those moments, instead of shoehorning them in later. Functionality can influence everything from kitchen layouts and socket positions to furniture choices and lighting options. Often it is what saves you money in the long run.

Timelessness and Longevity

By perfectly marrying form and function, Japandi interiors have a timeless appeal that defies fashions. Instead of just focusing on the aesthetics for immediate impact, it pays to take the time to consider the function of your home. Trends can come and go, but making the right choices for you is what will ensure that your home is future-proofed for the long term.

Since the mid-20th century, Scandinavian design has never really gone out of fashion. Instead, it has faced enduring popularity and respect from across the world, from both minimalists and maximalists alike. Scandinavian design can't really be described as trendy, in the same way that Japanese design can't be trivialized. They're both a representation of the values that both cultures hold dearly—namely craftsmanship, thoughtfulness, simplicity, and an affinity with nature. Each of those values has the aim of sustaining longevity. In that sense, these two philosophies have a rich heritage—their concept of design has been consistently refined and clarified to help bring new life to old ideas. It's what has made chairs designed one hundred years ago still popular today. With roots in both cultures, the Japandi approach, while a popular trend at the moment, can be said to have a sense of timelessness already built into it. Timeless design is part of the Japandi DNA.

Aesthetically, the minimal interiors of the Japandi style can be considered timeless because they're conservative and classic yet versatile. You can pair almost anything with a neutral backdrop and it will look right. It makes it much easier to quickly change up your accessories than having to paint a wall, for example. Then there's timelessness that comes with getting the function right. If you design for functionality and create a space that works for you, you're less likely to end up having to change things or replace items further down the

line, for example, if your sofa choice proves uncomfortable or you find your workspace isn't optimized. Mostly it's about taking a slower approach and not rushing into decisions. Spend time thinking about the reasoning behind everything and you're less likely to make mistakes. Ask yourself: Why do you like something? How practical is it? Will it still be suitable for you in a few years' time? Would it work somewhere else if you moved home?

HOW TO CREATE A TIMELESS SPACE

Comfort

True comfort and contentment in a space comes from both the body and mind—we need physical comfort, but we also need to feel at home in a space. When choosing a big-ticket item like a sofa or bed, try before you buy. We all have different bodies, which will influence the way we use a piece of furniture. For example, if you're fairly tall, you might need a sofa with a taller back to support your shoulders when you watch TV. If you like reading books on the sofa, you might want deeper arms to lean on.

Practicality

It's easy to get carried away with all the pretty things without considering the more pragmatic details of a space. You might like the idea of a cream sofa, but in reality you might have sticky fingers or muddy paws to deal with. You can still make that choice, but adapt the look to your circumstances, perhaps considering washable covers or a stain-resistant version. You're also more likely to want to use something if it works on a practical level.

Adaptability

If you were buying a new outfit, you might think about cost per wear and what else you could pair with it. The same goes for interiors—think about the different ways you can use items and if they might suit different rooms if you decided to move things around at a later date.

Simplicity

Simple forms tend to be more timeless because they're not defined by a particular era or style. Look for clean lines, unfussy details, and high-quality materials.

Cohesion

A cohesive home is one where there is a sense of visual connection between different rooms. The Scandinavians call this the "red thread"— it's a consistent theme or color that helps to tie everything together into a complete concept. When decorating, it helps to think in terms of repetition—you might use one element in one room then repeat it in different forms elsewhere. For example, if you paint a wall green in one room, you could use the same shade of green in your bathroom tiles or with your sofa cushions.

Suitability

A home will better stand the test of time if it is appropriate for its context. Consider the architecture of your home and be sensitive to the type of decoration that will suit the bones of what you're working with. For example, an industrial-style table might not necessarily fit with an Art Deco house.

Inclusivity

When making a decision, ask yourself whether it will suit everyone in your home, now and in the future. If you're thinking about getting pets, for instance, choose hard-wearing materials and scratch-resistant finishes. If you involve children in the creative process of designing or decorating their rooms, even if it's not quite to your taste, they're also more likely to use the space and hopefully look after it. You might also want to consider potential buyers if you're thinking about selling in the future—neutral interiors tend to have universal appeal.

Spatial Flexibility

The joy of having a minimalist space is that it is much easier to move furniture around and switch things up whenever you feel like it. Japandi interiors have adaptability built into them, meaning that spaces can slowly evolve and grow with the inhabitant. Having control over an interior allows you to create a sense of belonging and connection, where you can make a home completely your own.

Unlike in the West, traditional Japanese homes didn't have pre-defined rooms with specific functions, such as a dining room for eating or a living room for relaxing, conceived with a particular family unit in mind. Instead, versatility was key, and rooms were referred to by their size, not their purpose. The internal arrangement of a home was dictated entirely by each individual, not by set walls or fixed rooms. According to *The Essential Japanese House* by Teiji Itoh, homes were made to be completely adaptable so that the function of the spaces could be changed according to the desires of the owner or even the time of day or particular season. Japanese houses were typically constructed using a post-and-beam system, called *jikugumi*, which uses widely spaced wooden columns and beams to bear the load and form a structural framework that allows for the easy assembly and disassembly of moveable internal fixtures, called *zosaku*. The open space of a home could then be divided up as needed with lightweight partitions instead of solid walls, using translucent *shoji* screens to separate inside and out, and opaque *fusuma* screens to create internal "rooms." If someone else moved in later, it meant they could even take out a partition and combine several rooms into one big space if desired.

While homes have evolved since then, and we don't all have the possibility of such extreme versatility, there's a lot we can learn about designing a home to

support our own needs. A home should be in service to its owner, rather than the other way around. This is especially true in today's homes where we are asking for more from them than ever before—our homes are now our sanctuary and our office, as well as our very own spa, gym, restaurant, and home cinema. We might work from the dining table, our kids might do their homework at the kitchen island, and then we might want to shift everything around to entertain friends in the evening. Integrating open flexibility into a design can help to create longer-lasting spaces that work for all your needs, now and in the future.

HOW TO MAKE THE MOST OF A SMALL SPACE

Think of elevation as well as plan

If you're working with a small footprint, free up precious floor space and make use of the full height of your walls. Wall-mounted storage solutions won't intrude on a room as much as something that's more solid on the ground. For example, you could install a floor-to-ceiling shelving unit with a fold-out desk unit, or floating shelves either side of a bed if you don't have space for bedside tables. Don't forget the space above doorways too.

Lift furniture off the floor

Choose furniture on slender legs rather than bulky designs. Being able to see the floor running underneath a piece of furniture will give a greater illusion of space.

Less, but bigger

Instead of cramming a room with lots of small pieces, which can easily start to look cluttered, opt for fewer things but in generous sizes. Especially with rugs, choose the largest you think your room can take, so your furniture can mostly be placed on top of the rug. This gives a feeling of generosity to a space, rather than a rug floating in the middle of the room like an island.

Choose multipurpose furniture

Look for inventive designs that can easily adapt and serve different uses, while not taking up too much space, such as an extendable dining table or a footstool that conceals a single pull-out bed for a guest. Anything on wheels is also great for moving out of the way when needed.

Furniture with hidden storage

Maximize your storage possibilities, for example, with an ottoman bed that can lift up to reveal enough space to store spare bedding and even suitcases, or a coffee table that can hide ugly remotes.

The space under furniture

Don't forget underused spaces that can often get overlooked, for example, under a sofa or armchair. Use pull-out trays and baskets to store easily accessible children's toys, books, or magazines out of sight.

Blend in your storage

Paint any fitted furniture the same color as the walls so it becomes part of the architecture and fades into the background. This will mean that your eye won't be drawn to the bulky weight of a piece of storage.

Mirrors

Use mirrors to bounce light around and trick the eye into thinking a space is bigger than it actually is. Strategically position your mirrors to reflect the best views of your space.

Arranging art and accessories

Keep any decorative detail to set zones or areas in a room to prevent a space looking too crowded. And remember the negative space around an object is as important as the object itself.

Storage and Furniture

Japandi furniture is characterized by straight lines, box-like forms, and uncomplicated shapes. Designs are there to blend in and support everyday life, rather than clamor for attention. The secret to the minimalist look is plenty of storage so you can hide away the things you don't want to see on a daily basis, and only have out the things you really need.

When it comes to Japanese and Scandinavian furniture, often the beauty of a design will only come out through getting the function right first. If something is inherently functional, it's more likely to be naturally comfortable and appealing in its useability. Take, for example, a chair where the back has been ergonomically shaped to support the human spine; it makes sitting easier, but it also creates a streamlined shape that looks aesthetically pleasing. Japandi furniture is therefore not conceived for show homes or gallery spaces, but real, everyday homes that are designed to be used and cherished. By prioritizing functionality, Japandi designs tend to be simpler in form, because they have been reduced down to only what is necessary. The thinking is that embellishment isn't really needed if it doesn't serve a purpose, in fact, it could even detract from the object.

For Japanese and Scandinavian design, there was also a desire to be democratic, with a movement to create well-designed, everyday objects that could be used and appreciated by everyone. Japanese brand MUJI was founded in the 1980s with a collection of forty household objects that offered "all value, no frills." Based on values of form, function, and simplicity, MUJI has become known for their simple packaging and reasonably priced basics. In Sweden, IKEA had a similar effect, igniting our love of flat-pack furniture with the tagline "creating a better everyday life for the many people." Suddenly interior design wasn't just the preserve of elite designers; anyone could transform their home and create an impact.

A FLOOR-LEVEL LIFESTYLE

The concept of furniture design is relatively new in the history of Japanese design. In fact, before Japan opened up to trade with the West, homes didn't really have furniture at all, or not as we know it elsewhere in the world. This is because the Japanese have traditionally had a culture of sitting and living on the floor. If there was any furniture in the home, it might be the odd table, floor cushion, or a built-in wall shelf. Any designs would be low, simple, and often without legs, to be easily used from a sitting position. Before beds became more widely used, the Japanese would also sleep directly on the floor on tatami mats (a floor mat made from rice straw covered in rush grass) or slim futons, which could be folded and put to one side in the morning—and many people still do. There were multiple reasons for this—not only was sleeping on a firm surface said to be good for the back, but lightweight, moveable designs also allowed for greater flexibility in a space. Japanese homes were typically quite small, so a bedroom might need to be transformed into a living room by day and back again by night. Living with less also helped to cement the clean, minimalist aesthetic that prioritizes a feeling of spaciousness and openness.

According to the book *Traditional Japanese Furniture* by Kazuko Koizumi, chairs were first brought over to Japan from China, then later by missionaries and traders coming from Spain and Portugal in the 16th century. Then, they were only really used by the very rich. With a strong desire to preserve the unique culture, the Japanese were initially skeptical about the idea of chairs:

STORAGE IDEAS FOR JAPANDI SPACES

Built-in window seats

Create a restful corner with a deep, generous window seat to frame your favorite view outside. Whether it's an IKEA hack or something more bespoke, install a lift-up seat or drawers to make the most of storage space underneath.

Room dividers

An open shelving unit that runs from floor to ceiling can be installed between spaces to help zone different areas while still allowing views through and the free flow of light. Close off the bottom of the unit with cupboards if you need more practical storage rather than display space. Room dividers work especially well in homes where you walk straight into a living room and want to create the sense of privacy of a hallway.

Built-in floating shelves

Ideal for alcoves and smaller spaces, install wall-to-wall floating shelves to display your favorite objects. Having shelves instead of wall cabinets in a kitchen can also help to give a feeling of spaciousness.

A bed with storage

Maximize storage in a small bedroom by building floor-to-ceiling closets either side of a bed with cupboard units above where the headboard would be. Create a ledge behind the bed for books or a glass of water, and integrate bedside lights for a boutique hotel look.

Picture ledges

These are narrow shelves that can be used to curate an ever-changing display of picture frames, design books, and keepsakes.

Walk-in closet cupboards

In bigger bedrooms, create a separate walk-in closet by placing cupboard joinery in the middle of the room or directly behind a headboard, with a route through on either side.

A Murphy bed

Where space is extremely tight or you're looking for a multifunctional solution, consider a space-saving Murphy bed, which is stored upright as part of the wall when not in use and can be pulled down with a piston mechanism when needed.

Kitchen cabinet that reach the ceiling

Traditional kitchen cabinets tend to stop just short of the ceiling, but this wasted space often just ends up gathering dust. It creates a more seamless look if joinery meets the ceiling, not to mention being more practical.

Door reveals

Add depth to spaces by building shelving for books around and above doorways.

A dining bench

Create a built-in dining bench on one side of your dining table. Not only will it create more comfortable banquette-style seating, but you'll also benefit from plenty of hidden storage below.

"When chairs did find their way to Japan, it was always as curious objects out of cultural context. There was no real connection to the person who made them ... and chairs remained precious toys for the few; decorative items that never found their way into the daily life of the people." That was until the 20th century, when Western furniture trends and a taste for modernism came over from Europe, paving the way for simple wooden furniture with a distinctly Nordic influence.

This was a completely new way of living for the Japanese—even just the idea of sitting and eating at a table was novel. Having never had the need for chairs, the manufacturing industry was unprepared and mostly used to making cabinets and shelving units. In the book *Japanese Design Since 1945*, Makoto Shimazaki notes that the Japanese took Danish furniture as their example—in order to not only modernize and create goods to export, but also to serve the growing fashion for Western-style interiors in Japan itself. Furniture brand Karimoku says that even now the Japanese furniture industry is dictated by European aesthetics, and often the size of designs have to be adapted for the European or American market.

While fashions have changed, there is something appealing about the Japanese floor-level lifestyle. It brings you closer to Earth, creating a grounding feeling that connects you to your surroundings. It somehow feels like a more natural way to inhabit a space than sitting on formal furniture that dictates how you should position your body. In that way it brings us back to our roots. And it's likely better for our bodies too—we know that sitting in one position thanks to today's modern sedentary lifestyles can cause all sorts of aches, pains, and strains, especially if it's in front of a computer. Sitting or kneeling on the floor, on the other hand, can help with flexibility, movement, and posture. Even if you don't give up chairs or a comfy sofa completely, just having a few floor cushions or poufs can help create a more informal feel, which invites guests to kick off their shoes and relax. You could also consider a platform or floor bed to fully embrace the floor-level lifestyle.

KARIMOKU FURNITURE

Karimoku Furniture is one of the biggest furniture manufacturers in Japan. With a respect for the timeless beauty of nature, the brand's heritage is deeply connected to its main material of choice: wood.

Having inherited a lumber business, founder Shohei Kato set up a small woodworking shop in Aichi Prefecture in 1940, first creating wooden packaging boxes then sewing-machine tables, pianos, and TV stands for the domestic Japanese market. The name Karimoku is made up of *Kari*, which derives from Kato's hometown of Kariya, and *moku*, taken from the Japanese word for wood, *mokuzai*. Conscious of the changing times and evolving tastes, the company

worked hard to modernize its woodworking techniques and soon transitioned into creating its own brand of original furniture in the 1960s.

Karimoku's furniture is still made in Japan, using a "High Tech, High Touch" approach that combines the handmade finish of expert craftsmanship with the precision of cutting-edge production and technical innovation. Every design is formed of wood, in some shape or form, with the belief that it is the workers' hands that draw out the inherent beauty in the natural grain of the material. It takes two years to fully train and gain enough skills to make a straightforward sofa, and everything is quality-checked by hand, down to the last detail. Karimoku Furniture mostly uses locally sourced oak from Japan or imported cherry or walnut, which is dried on-site at their factory. Karimoku's designs are made to last and are designed to be used every day—highly customizable machinery allows them to use advanced ergonomics to create items that work for the human body and will stand up to wear. They've typically found that their Japanese customers value function and versatility in their furniture, preferring perfect finishes and a thick layer of hard-wearing varnish, while their European audience seems to be more open to little imperfections in the wood, such as knots, scars, and cracks.

Today, Karimoku Furniture is bringing Japanese design into the future by collaborating with a new generation of European designers such as Norm Architects (see interview, pages 60–63). Karimoku Case Study, for instance, is a collection of bespoke wooden furniture conceived by Norm Architects and Keiji Ashizawa (see interview, pages 156–159) that seamlessly fuses Japanese and Scandinavian influences. Each piece is designed for a specific architectural project, with the philosophy that furniture should be in harmony with its surroundings in order to create a comfortable setting for all the senses.

Layout

Creating a functional home comes down to how we interact with our surroundings. Getting the layout right will mean that journeys through a space are optimized and there's a sense of flow between different areas. Whether you embrace open-plan living or want to unite a series of smaller spaces, a Japandi home should feel instantly intuitive to use.

When it comes to planning an interior project, a key piece of the puzzle is creating a comfortable, functional layout. You need to feel like you can move through a space easily and not meet any awkward junctions. Also consider maximizing views and draw attention to a room's best focal points. A Japandi interior has an airy, spacious quality that makes it feel like you could just float through a room unencumbered. Often there's plenty of free space between objects, allowing pieces of furniture to breathe and be taken in slowly by the eye. Aesthetics obviously play a role, but this use of careful restraint helps to create that tranquil, restful feel. The Japanese have a concept called *ma* (see page 53), which is the idea of negative space, and applies not only to the physical presence of a gap between things but the perception or feeling of space too. In an interior space, *ma* gives purpose to the empty corners, so furniture is carefully placed to create moments of controlled focus. It's not about creating wasted space or having so little that a room feels cold and soulless, but creating a balance between openness and coziness.

There are several ways that you can plan the layout of your home. You could sketch out a plan of your room on a piece of graph paper and cut out smaller pieces to represent furniture, shifting them around by hand until you get something that works. There are also various digital layout tools, such as SketchUp, which you can download for free and use quite easily, even if you

have no design background. Another clever trick is to mark out the outline of any potential furniture directly on the floor with masking tape to get an instant representation of how big something might be. It will take a bit of trial and error but often it will feel like something just clicks when you get the layout right.

ZONING

Another clever spatial planning technique you can use, called zoning, gives a distinct feel or purpose to different areas within the same open plan space. It helps to organize an internal layout and create a sense of separation between various functions, such as eating, cooking, socializing, and relaxing. You can use solid partitions to more obviously zone and compartmentalize spaces, such as with half walls, room dividers, sliding panels, and open shelves, but zoning also comes down to the position of your furniture and decorative choices. Rugs are an easy way to delineate spaces effectively, while the backs of sofas can be used to create routeways behind them and direct views from one area to another. You could also use contrasting floor finishes or color blocking, which is where you use a bold section of color to create the visual effect of separating off a space.

SCALE AND PROPORTION

As well as the space between objects and furniture, you also need to consider the size of objects in relation to one another as well as in relation to the area of the room. It can create a sense of imbalance if items are out of proportion with each other, not to mention be impractical, for example, if you had a coffee table that was too tall for your sofa or if your bedside tables were so low that it was awkward to reach down to them.

Japandi interiors tend to have a very human scale, meaning that items don't feel imposing or overbearing, but well-considered to work with the dimensions of the human form. First, take into account the size of the room and the ceiling height, making sure to choose furniture that fits comfortably in that setting with plenty of room to spare. If you have lower ceilings, opt for furniture that is lower to the ground to help emphasize a sense of height. Think about how the style of your furniture can fit in too—if you have ornate detailing in a room, you might choose a more slender sofa, but if your space is more modern with boxy proportions, a chunky modular sofa might be a better fit. Most importantly, ensure that you can move around your key pieces of furniture easily. With smaller items and accessories, try to match their size so everything feels like a natural fit. For example, a table lamp with a shade that is no bigger than the side table it's on, or an armchair with the same height seat and back as your sofa. An exception is pendant lighting, where you can be a bit more generous with its size, helping to create impact in a space. The Japanese are particularly skilled at using oversized paper pendants to bring a soft glow to a room. Remember that the Japandi style values asymmetry, so not everything has to mirror each other. You can keep objects in scale with one another, but break it up with a subtle note of differentiation, for example with mismatched dining chairs, an art print positioned to one side of a sofa, or different lamps either side of a bed.

MODULAR DESIGN

Traditionally, the Japanese didn't use the metric or imperial system to measure their interiors or homes. Instead they used a standardized modular system that defined the size of tatami mats, *fusuma* sliding doors, and *shoji* screens, ensuring everything fitted together efficiently. A structure was defined by a unit of measurement called a *ken,* which is more or less the height of a typical person, making a tatami mat approximately 1 *ken* by 0.5 *ken,* the perfect size for someone to sleep on. Because tatami mats were used to cover the whole floor surface of a space, rooms were typically described according to how many mats they could hold, for example a 6-tatami mat room. Tatami mats come in set sizes, but these vary according to region. A Kyoto tatami mat

is slightly bigger than a Tokyo tatami mat, for example. This old systemization meant that architects or builders could scale up a space and know that any interior elements would always fit and be in proportion to one another.

A SENSE OF FLOW

The idea of flow in interior design describes the sense of fluidity and harmony you feel when you move from one space to another. A room can have visual flow, where everything works together to complement each other, but it should also have to a physical feeling of flow, which is all about routes through a space. It helps to think about the journeys you make when doing certain tasks in a room. For example, in the kitchen you should aim to create a "golden triangle" between the oven, fridge, and sink, so that your route is the most efficient and you're not making wasted journeys going from one side of the room to the other. Often it can help to draw route lines directly onto a plan of your space, so you can easily see how you might come into a space and move about in it. Make sure furniture isn't blocking off movement or preventing you from getting around in a fluid motion. In smaller spaces, curved edges can help to create a better sense of flow.

Practical Beauty

AN INTERVIEW WITH KODA MUNETOSHI, DIRECTOR OF KOYORI

Launched in 2022, KOYORI is a Japanese design brand that collaborates with contemporary designers from across the world to create furniture that showcases the heritage and aesthetics of Japanese craftsmanship. The brand identity was formed under the direction of British designer Jasper Morrison, and the brand has worked with Paris-based brothers Ronan and Erwan Bouroullec, Danish–Italian duo GamFratesi, and London-based Michael Anastassiades. Here Koda Munetoshi, executive director of KOYORI, explains how function underpins the foundations of Japanese design.

Can you tell me about KOYORI's aim to "transcend borders"?

We are trying to create something that is borderless, which means it's not Japanese, it's not European, it could be from anywhere. Our goal is to make design that is really useful for everyday life. But the real reason why we established KOYORI is that we wanted to support Japanese furniture manufacturers. Even though we have so many in Japan—about 6,000 furniture manufacturers and that's not including the smaller workshops—only a few manufacturers have had the chance to infiltrate their own brand into the international market. We have a wealth of craftsmanship and manufacturing skills in this country, but often there's a lack of resources, whether that's a language barrier or a lack of expertise in logistics or marketing. We didn't have a plan to help the manufacturers individually because the scale of the manufacture is still too small. So that's why we invited a couple of the top manufacturers from across Japan to form an alliance.

Then we had to think about the design. The products had to be really useful and functional for the people who are going to use them. We wanted to promote Japanese craftsmanship, but that didn't mean that we wanted to introduce Japanese design. That's why we decided to invite some designers from Europe.

How did you choose the European designers you wanted to work with?

For the first collection we invited Ronan and Erwan Bouroullec from France, then GamFratesi, who are based in Copenhagen. Often traditional Japanese manufacturers can be conservative. But these designers are so good at always creating something new. Every time they design something, they bring a new way of thinking. GamFratesi have a great talent for editing and making use of an old technique or an old piece of heritage, but giving it a new value.

How does the collaboration process usually work?

It was actually a tough mission because everything happened during the Covid-19 pandemic. It was a really weird time. Right after the first meeting with Ronan, I flew back to Japan, and everything was shut down. It was tricky; we would film the manufacturers at work as much as possible and explain details to the designers, such as what they specialized in. Finally one year later they could come and visit.

What do you think is the role of functionality in Japanese design?

This is just my personal opinion—I'm not a designer—but I think there are two reasons why functionalism is important to Japanese people. First of all, we have a long-held belief that a product must be durable and useful for everyday life. Then, we believe that real, effective beauty results from that functionalism. We tend to think that if something is functional then it is beautiful. If it's not functional, it's not beautiful. Because a product should be for the everyday, not something you put in the corner of the room and don't actually use. That's why the Japanese people believe function needs to come first before the aesthetic. And if you try to obtain the ultimate level of function, it's got to be simple—then it's going to be automatically beautiful.

Do you think that's also because the Japanese see design in everything, even mundane objects?

Another reason is probably that, for a long time, the idea of the designer was really unpopular in Japan. Objects were made by anonymous people. Even if a carpenter was famous in his industry, ninety-nine percent of Japanese people wouldn't have known who they were. They would make anonymous products that were useful. But because that product was designed by people who weren't famous, there was no royalty or reward system. That's why the price was reasonable, and everybody could purchase these items. That was what created a sense of nonhierarchy in this country.

Why do you think there is such affinity between Japanese and Scandinavian design?

After the idea of functionality, we also have a commonality with the use of natural wood. Wood was a really, really important material for the Japanese people, and coincidentally, the Scandinavians also had a great amount of forest. Automatically, we developed a similar technique for working with wood. Simplicity is required to produce beautiful wooden products, so then naturally the designs ended up becoming similar. But the important thing is, why was wood so important for the Japanese people? A total of seventy percent of our land is covered in forest, so wood became a common material for everybody and was used for everything, not only furniture but dishes, chopsticks, and spoons. In Japan we also have the idea of animism, where we believe that there is a god in everything; in the rivers, mountains, and trees. We have a legend that God actually used a tall tree as a ladder when he came down to Earth. Gradually, the Japanese people started believing that there is a spirit in trees. That's why when craftspeople or carpenters produce something, they really want to use wood.

Do you notice any differences between Japanese and Scandinavian design?

The Japanese finishes are more shiny, but on the other hand, the Scandinavian people prefer the lightly oiled finish because it's more natural and you feel the grain. They also don't mind that it patinates and gets more character. The Japanese people are more meticulous. If they spill some coffee, and it creates a stain, it's more of a big deal. That's why the Japanese people started asking the manufacturers to protect the products with more hard-wearing finishes, and they began to use the lacquer finish.

Why do you think Scandinavian design has so appealed to the Japanese?

I don't know, but in the 1990s we had an explosion with the Bubble economy and started having recessions. People seemed to want something that was really gentle and soft, and the Scandinavian culture, with its importance of light, felt like a gentle culture with a soft atmosphere. It felt really heartwarming. The natural material palette was also really well received by Japanese homes.

Finally, what does functionality mean to KOYORI?

Simplicity is really beautiful and at the same time kind of functional. There is another concept in Japanese design called *yonobi*. *Yo* means "practical," *no* means "of," and *bi* means "beauty," so beauty of the practical; practical beauty. It was a phrase created by one of Japan's most famous craftspeople, Soetsu Yanagi. Often people misunderstand *yonobi* and think it means functional. But strictly speaking, *yonobi* doesn't quite mean function first. Of course, function is necessary for the products, but at the same time, unless a product is beautiful, it's not going to attract the user. They might get bored with it and then they're going to switch products pretty quickly. That's why *yonobi* means that a product must be practical, but it must also be aesthetic. That's real *yonobi*. We're trying to create something related to *yonobi*, which can represent both the functional and the beautiful.

Further Reading

Books

Ciorra, Pippo, and Florence Ostende, eds. *The Japanese House: Architecture and Life After 1945*. Marsilio Editori, 2017.

Dunn, Michael. *Traditional Japanese Design: Fives Tastes*. Abrams, 2001.

Gelfer-Jorgensen, Mirjam. *Influences from Japan: in Danish Art and Design 1870–2010*. Arkitektens Forlag, 2022.

Ilda, Mihoko. *Japanese Interiors*. Phaidon Press, 2022.

Itoh, Teiji. *The Essential Japanese House*. Weatherhill/Harper & Row, 1967.

Juniper, Andrew. *Wabi Sabi: The Japanese Art of Impermanence*. Tuttle Publishing, 2003.

Kemske, Bonnie. *Kintsugi: The Poetic Mend*. Herbert Press, 2021.

Koizumi, Kazuko. *Traditional Japanese Furniture*. Kodansha America, Inc., 1986.

Koren, Leonard. *Wabi-Sabi for Artists, Designers, Poets and Philosophers*. Imperfect Publishing, 2008.

Kries, Mateo, and Jochen Eisenbrand. *Alvar Aalto: Second Nature*. Vitra Design Museum, 2014.

Longhurst, Niimi. *Japonisme: Ikigai, Forest Bathing, Wabi-Sabi and More*. Harper Thorsons, 2018.

Menegazzo, Rossella. *Iro: The Essence of Colour in Japanese Design*. Phaidon Press, 2022.

——, and Stefania Piotti. *Wa: The Essence of Japanese Design*. Phaidon Press, 2014.

Miyazaki, Yoshifumi. *Walking in the Woods: Go back to nature with the Japanese way of shinrin-yoku*. Aster, 2021.

Navarro, Tomás. *Kintsugi: Embrace Your Imperfections and Find Happiness—The Japanese Way*. Yellow Kite, 2018.

Norm Architects. *Stillness*. Gestalten, 2024.

PIE International and Kumiko Ishii. *Machiya: The Traditional Townhouses of Kyoto*. 2020.

Pollock, Naomi. *Japanese Design Since 1945: A Complete Sourcebook*. Thames & Hudson, 2020.

Russell, Helen. *The Year of Living Danishly*. Icon Books, 2015.

Satoh, Taku. *Just Enough Design*. Chronicle Books, 2022.

Seike, Kiyosi. *The Art of Japanese Joinery*. Weatherhill Inc., 1997.

Tanizaki, Junichiro. *In Praise of Shadows*. Penguin, 2019.

Weisberg, Gabriel P., Anna-Maria von Bonsdorff, and Hanne Selkokari, eds. *Japanomania in the Nordic Countries 1875–1918*. Yale University Press, 2016.

Wiking, Meik. *The Little Book of Hygge: The Danish Way to Live Well*. Penguin, 2016.

Yanagi, Soetsu. *The Unknown Craftsman: A Japanese Insight Into Beauty*. Kodansha America, Inc., 2013.

——. *The Beauty of Everyday Things*. Penguin, 2019.

Essays and Articles

Chiu, Chen-Yu, Aino Niskanen, and Ke Song. "Humanizing Modern Architecture." *Journal of Asian Architecture and Building Engineering*, October 24, 2018, tandfonline.com/doi/pdf/10.3130/jaabe.16.1.

Crossley-Baxter, Lily. "Japan's Ancient Way to Save the Planet." BBC Travel, March 9, 2020, bbc.com/travel/article/20200308-japans-ancient-way-to-save-the-planet.

Fries, Kevin. "Five Mono No Aware." In *In the Province of the Gods* (University of Wisconsin Press, 2017): 46–54.

Harvey, Ailsa, and Alina Bradford. "The Five (and More) Human Senses." Live Science, June 10, 2024, .livescience.com/60752-human-senses.html

"Japanese Aesthetics of Shadow and Darkness." *Kogei Standard*, April 19, 2023, kogeistandard.com/insight/serial/editor-in-chief-column-kogei/inei.

"Kami." BBC, September 4, 2009, bbc.co.uk/religion/religions/shinto/beliefs/kami_1.shtml.

Lomas, T., et al. "The Art of Living Mindfully." *Journal of Religion and Health* (2017), repository.uel.ac.uk.

Mitsuhashi, Yukari. "Ikigai: A Japanese Concept to Improve Work and Life." BBC Worklife, August 8, 2017, bbc.com/worklife/article/20170807-ikigai-a-japanese-concept-to-improve-work-and-life.

"Scandinavian Design: Everything You Need to Know." Scandanavia Standard, scandinaviastandard.com/what-is-scandinavian-design/.

Shibata, Seiji, and Naoto Suzuki. "Effects of the Foliage Plant on Task Performance and Mood." *Journal of Environmental Psychology* 22, no. 3 (2022): 262–72.

Tanmoy Das, Lala. "What Science Tells Us About the Mood-Boosting Effects of Indoor Plants." *Washington Post*, July 7, 2022.

"The Philosophy Behind the Japanese Art Form of Kintsugi." The Conversation, November 8, 2022, theconversation.com/how-the-philosophy-behind-the-japanese-art-form-of-kintsugi-can-help-us-navigate-failure-193487.

"What is Hygge?" denmark.dk/people-and-culture/hygge.

"Why Living Near Forests is Good for Your Brain." World Economic Forum, October 23, 2017, weforum.org/agenda/2017/10/living-near-forests-is-good-for-your-brain/.

Index

Credits

2 Ariake; **6** Anna Cor; **8** Renee Kemps for Maana Homes; **11** Cate St Hill; **12** Cate St Hill; **15** Nordic Knots – Jute Corner rug, from £345 at nordicknots.com; **16** T-Lamp and Sintra table by FRAMA; **17** Avenue Design Studio; **19** Niki Brantmark/My Scandinavian Home; **21** Mia Borgelin; **23** Merö Studio; **25** Blue Dela Cruz @niblu.home; **26** Design: Laura Logan of House of Logan, photography: Sarah Button; **29** Niki Brantmark/My Scandinavian Home; **30** Design: Laura Logan of House of Logan, photography: Helen Leech; **31** Avenue Design Studio; **33** Mikael Lundblad; **35** Norm Architects – Archipelago House, photography: Jonas Bjerre-Poulsen; **39** Karl Anderson/Living4Media; Verdenius Photography; **40** Marianne Jacobsen; **43** Norm Architects – Skovshoved Residence, photography: Jonas Bjerre-Poulsen; **47** Tomohiro Kenken for Keiji Ashizawa Design; **48** Anna Cor; **51** Kristofer Johnsson; **52** Norm Architects – Forest Retreat, photography: Jonas Bjerre-Poulsen; **53** Verdenius Photography; **55** Interior design: Nordy Study, photography: Dovaldé Buténaité; **56** Blue Dela Cruz @niblu.home; **58** Isle glassware range by FRAMA; **63** Norm Architects – Skovshoved Residence, photography: Jonas Bjerre-Poulsen; **64** Kubus candleholder by Audo Copenhagen. Photography: Jonas Bjerre-Poulsen/Norm Architects; **67** Interior design: Marie-Astrid Pelsser, furniture: Desiron Lizen, photo: CaroLine Dethier; **69** Stool 60 by Alvar Aalto from Artek, available from Artek 2nd Cycle; **70** Cate St Hill; **73** Offset bedspread by ferm LIVING; **75** Avenue Design Studio; **77** Shibori Clay wall covering in pale beige, belarteSTUDIO; **79** Courtesy of Marimekko. Photography by Mikko Ryhänen; **81** POJ Studio; **82** POJ Studio; **87** Renee Kemps for Maana Homes; **88** Norm Architects & Karimoku Case – Kinuta Terrace, photography: Jonas Bjerre-Poulsen; **91** Norm Architects – Forest Retreat, photography: Jonas Bjerre-Poulsen; **92** Cate St Hill; **95** Norm Architects – Heatherhill Beach House, photography: Jonas Bjerre-Poulsen; **96** Cate St Hill; **99** Cate St Hill; **100** hsfoto/Living4Media; **103** Cate St Hill; **105** Norm Architects – Forest Retreat, photography: Jonas Bjerre-Poulsen; **109** Armchair 45 in Natural Linen Webbing by Alvar Aalto from Artek, available from artek.fi; **110** Courtesy of Bemz. Styling: Annaleena Leino, photography: Kristofer Johnsson; **113** Project: Mon Projects, interior design: Daytrip, photography: Jake Curtis; **114** Cate St Hill; **116** Cate St Hill; **118** Styling: Kate Imogen Wood, photography: Stine Christiansen; **120** Are Media/Living4Media; **121** Rico lounge chair by ferm LIVING in the home of Mikkel Dahlstrøm; **122** Jocke Ono; **123** Kirsty Dawn/Vertone; **125** Tarn dining table by ferm LIVING; **126** Ask og Eng Design; **120** Image courtesy of Graen Studios. Ceramic bowl by Yellow Nose Studio; **131** Interior design: TE-EL, photography: Studio Periphery; **135** &Tradition; **136** Norm Architects – Heatherhill Beach House, photography: Jonas Bjerre-Poulsen; **139** Ask og Eng Design; **141** Norm Architects – Heatherhill Beach House, photography: Jonas Bjerre-Poulsen; **143** Ask og Eng Design; **144** Norm Architects – Forest Retreat, photography: Jonas Bjerre-Poulse; **147** Walls painted in "Lulling" by Atelier Ellis. Photography: Kalina Krawczyk; **149** Cate St Hill; **151** Cate St Hill; **153** India Hobson for TOAST; **154** Verdenius Photography; **157** Jonas Bjerre-Poulsen for Keiji Ashizawa Design; **160** Interior design: TE-EL, photography: Studio Periphery; **163** Cate St Hill; **164** Nordiska Kök; **167** Cate St Hill; **168** Julia Cawley/Living4Media; **171** Tomooki Kengaku for Keiji Ashizawa Design; **172** Ståle Eriksen; **174** &Tradition; **176** Sandie Lykke Nolsøe for Karimoku Case; **179** Cate St Hill; **180** Sandie Lykke Nolsøe for Karimoku Case; **181** Ask og Eng Design; **183** Jonas Bjerre-Poulsen for Keiji Ashizawa Design; **185** Cate St Hill.